Table of Contents

APPENDIX

KENNEDY'S

POCKET GUIDE

TO WORKING WITH

EXECUTIVE

RECRUITERS

KENNEDY PUBLICATIONS

Compiled and published by Kennedy Information
publishers of **Executive Recruiter News, Directory of Executive Recruiters, SearchSelect,
Directory of Outplacement Firms, Consultants News**
and **Directory of Management Consultants.**

One Kennedy Place, Route 12 South, Fitzwilliam, NH 03447

Phone: 603-585-6544
Fax: 603-585-9555
E-mail: bookstore@kennedyinfo.com
Internet: http://www.kennedyinfo.com

Library of Congress Catalog Card Number 73-642226
ISBN #1-885922-09-4

About this Guide . . .

When our first *Directory of Executive Recruiters* was published in 1971, it was a rather thin 52-page booklet plainly listing some 450 firms.

By the second edition, however, we were beginning to recognize the need to provide some guidance on how to use the list, how to work with the recruiters. Our response was a single page of text outlining a few cautions!

Over the years we have continuously expanded and refined this text portion: it grew to over 100 pages of helpful information from a wide variety of sources.

But with the entire directory at over 900 pages, and more than 1½ inches thick, we were approaching the physical limits of binding in paperback form.

Besides, we found that many directory purchasers skipped directly to the listings and missed all the up-front text! And purchasers of the listings in our new disk format wouldn't be getting the text at all. So we decided to separate the how-to-use information from the search firm listings and their extensive cross-indexes. Thus was born this new companion to *The Directory of Executive Recruiters.*

This "pocket" guide has essentially taken that earlier introductory text and added to it considerably. There are over 30 chapters covering, we hope, the gamut of information and guidance needed. We are especially appreciative of the cooperation of our authors, who have made this unique publication possible, and we welcome comments and suggestions from job-changers to help us make the next edition even better.

James H. Kennedy
Publisher

Fitzwilliam, NH
April, 1996

Call a Recruiting Organization by Any Other Name and It's Still a Recruiting Organization

by Robert Half

Filling jobs for companies, large and small, is a big industry, and there are many different ways to describe the segments of that industry. There are executive recruiters, personnel recruiters, personnel agencies, personnel services, etc. To take the extreme example, there is technically very little difference between an employment agency and an executive recruiting service—by definition. Both categories fill jobs. One specializes in routine jobs and may charge the job candidate if the employer will not pay the fee (this is a rarity these days). The other fills executive positions, and all fees and expenses are paid by the client. Customarily there is also a non-refundable retainer, paid in advance.

A personnel recruiter is more likely to be a specialist in an occupation or industry than is an executive recruiter, and its fees are paid by the client. But the executive recruiter does specialize in the highest level employees, such as CEOs—but may also be involved with mid-management positions as well. That is the point where there is the greatest overlap between the executive recruiter and the personnel recruiter. It's to the job candidate's advantage to investigate all opportunities, regardless of what the service is called.

The Choice Is Yours—But Be Careful

There are excellent doctors, lawyers and accountants—and there are some who are questionable, to say the least. The same is true in personnel services. Even though the job candidate does not generally pay them a fee, they may misguide candidates by reason of incompetency or anxiety to fill a position—without regard to ethics. (Certainly not common, but there are enough of them out there to be concerned.)

Separating the good from the not so good is a matter of keeping your eyes open and trusting your instincts. The better ones have been around for quite awhile, and they have on staff experienced personnel in the specialty you're interested in.

One way to find out which services tend to specialize in your occupation is to study the employment advertising in your local newspaper, trade publications and *The Wall Street Journal,* or its sister publication the *National Business Employment Weekly.*

People who are searching for jobs but are in no hurry to make a change can rely on one selected personnel recruiter. If the candidate is out-of-work, or his or her job is in jeopardy, it's wise to deal with all suitable recruiters. And, for that matter, all other sources.

In my book, *How to Get a Better Job in This Crazy World,* (Plume) I created an acronym: C.A.R.T.

C = Contacts. Use your network, and expand on it.
A = Advertising. Answer all appropriate ads, and consider placing position wanted ads.
R = Recruiters. As many suitable ones as possible
T = Temporary services. Many job-seekers have been recruited by the client of a temporary service—just because they were able to see a competent employee in action.

In answer to a common question: What's the best way to get a job? The answer is simple. Do everything at the same time and follow up every lead.

How to Get Recruiters to Work Harder for You

I could probably summarize it in two words, "be nice." Respect the recruiter's time—and also yours. Chatting for the sake of chatting doesn't help you or the placement manager—both of you should be busy. I'm not suggesting that you don't talk with each other—just make it short.

Keep the recruiter informed of your progress in job interviews that the recruiter sends you on. At the same time, you may receive pertinent information to guide you on further interviews. Perhaps the recruiter can give you status information, or further advice.

Read Before You Sign

There are certain forms that most personnel services will ask you to sign. Some are in your interest, others are not. Some are required by law—as an example, forms and procedures to prove that you have the right to work in the United States. And, without your signature, recruiters are forbidden by law to check out references. Refusing to sign this form will cut down on the opportunities you'll have a chance to explore. If you're currently employed, and your employer doesn't know you're looking, you should sign the reference form with the understanding that no current references can be checked at this time.

Standard application forms should be filled out completely, even if the information is covered in a resume. Placement people are accustomed to look for certain information, from time to time, and it's a lot easier for them to find it on your application than searching for it on a resume.

Most recruiters never charge candidates a fee regardless of what may happen later. Example: Some expect a fee if a job applicant accepts a job through the recruiting service, and then changes his or her mind. Or if you quit in a month or two, and they were not fully paid by the company. I'm not saying you should never sign any forms relating to the payment of a fee. Just understand what you're signing.

Career Counselors

Be careful. There are experienced specialists who are competent, ethical and honest. And there are others, some of whom made headline news. Make sure you get references, make sure you actually meet the person who is counseling you, and have a look at his or her resume. Don't read between-the-lines that they have contacts, expect their connections will get you a job. Perhaps? More likely not.

Robert Half is the founder of Robert Half International Inc., established in 1948 and listed on the New York Stock Exchange. His most recent book, published late 1993: Finding, Hiring and Keeping the Best Employees, *John Wiley & Sons.*

Some Ethical and Professional Aspects of the Executive Search Process

by Thomas H. Hall, former Chairman, Association of Executive Search Consultants (AESC)

The challenge of change offers executive job-changers many opportunities:

- It can be a time for in-depth self-assessment and evaluation to determine how best to use one's talents and abilities.
- It can be the chance to take a different course, fulfill an ambition, or make an impact in a new area.
- It can offer the opportunity to take on new responsibilities and discover new strengths and new resources.

During this sensitive and critical period it is important to be concerned with the standards and normal procedures of individuals and organizations in whom you place your trust.

Here are just a few of the aspects of the AESC search process of which you should be aware, and many are dealt with at greater length elsewhere in this Pocket Guide:

- Search consultants are retained to fill *bona-fide executive vacancies.* In other words, consultants recruit people for jobs. As such, no consultant should take your background information or resume and send it to an organization unless that consultant is working on a specific assignment. When you as a candidate send an unsolicited resume to a search firm, such information is reviewed and retained for appropriateness relative to future search assignments. You probably won't be contacted unless your qualifications match search specifications underway.
- The search process requires consultants to *meet with clients* to develop understanding of the client's organi-

zation, needs and position to be filled. Written documentation of the position is provided, and independent research on the client's industry is begun. A comprehensive search for qualified candidates and an evaluation of potential candidates is then undertaken. This process includes in-depth interviews and verification of the candidate's credentials. Comprehensive reference checking is conducted either before or after the candidate is presented to the client, but before a final selection has been made.

- *Confidentiality* is the distinguishing mark of a professional executive search consultant, and candidates can be assured that all information shared in the search process is held in confidence. If you are being considered, your availability will not be discussed without your permission.

- A significant value of an executive search is the *objectivity* that the consultant brings to the task. It is the consultant who assesses the fit between candidate and client's requirements, and upon whose recommendation the client relies. The threefold relationship between client, candidate and consultant must be characterized by candor and honesty. When honesty breaks down in any sector, the process is seriously impeded. Candidates, therefore, have a responsibility to be honest about their credentials, experiences and qualifications. They must make full disclosure to the consultant of their present situation, goals and ambitions. Candidates are also expected to maintain confidentiality about the specifics of the search, the company and information acquired.

- Every candidate desires a successful, satisfying experience in the relationship with a search consultant. If the interaction is marked by honesty, confidentiality and mutual respect, it can grow into a trusting, long-term relationship which will continue to benefit the executive and his or her company.

The Association of Executive Search Consultants (AESC) is the professional organization representing the executive search industry: each member firm has agreed to honor and be guided by the high standards of the profession. Some AESC firms are generalists, some specialize. Some are very large, with offices throughout the U.S. and the world. Some are small, and some are medium-sized.

Whatever their size or specialty, they all adhere to the AESC Code of Ethics and Professional Practice Guidelines. The AESC mission is to establish, maintain and enforce the highest professional standards in executive search consulting. The Association provides a system for investigating complaints that member firms have failed to adhere to these standards, and either client or candidate may complain if these standards are questioned. Appropriate disciplinary action is taken against member firms when the AESC Board determines that such complaints are justified.

Executive Search consultancy is a highly valued, respected component of management consulting—increasingly serving businesses and organizations worldwide—so it is extremely important that all participants in the process adhere to the highest ethical standards.

Thomas H. Hall, III, former chairman of the Association of Executive Search Consultants, is managing director for the Southeast Region of Korn/Ferry International, based in Atlanta. He joined the firm in 1978 after many years in higher education and investment banking, and he chairs his firm's Professional Practices and Training Committee.

Planning Your Career Search: The Four Major Strategies

by James F. Mohar

There are four, and only four, major search strategies, and each can be used at any time during the job-changing process:

1. Contact executive search firms.
2. Network with family, friends, acquaintances and business contacts.
3. Contact "target firms" of potential interest.
4. Reply to position available listings in newspapers, association and university publications, etc.

Warning: Don't just jump into the process and "get busy": it's extremely important to take time out for planning. Your search will probably take longer than you think—and what worked for someone else may not work for you—so if one, two, or three of the four search strategies are eliminated from consideration at the outset, a potentially career-making opportunity could be choked off.

It makes sense to consider using all four strategies and, if possible, concurrently, during the search process. Each one may produce interviews and, eventually, an offer.

The use of the four search strategies, and the balance it provides, is similar to the concept of financial asset diversification. Investment advisors point to portfolio diversification as a technique to provide balance between return and risk. In much the same way, using all four search strategies simultaneously helps uncover employment opportunities that otherwise would be missed.

1. CONTACT EXECUTIVE SEARCH FIRMS

There's no better ego stroke than to be "found" by a recruiter conducting a search on behalf of a corporate client.

But you can't wait for the telephone to ring: contact search firms directly. Unless you know the recruiter personally, the most effective method is to send a well-worded one-page cover letter with your resume.

Advantages

- *Quick Hit*—A resume reaching the right recruiter at the right time can result in an immediate interview. Timing and candidate/client compatibility relative to the position being filled are the crucial factors.
- *Shelf Life*—More so than any other strategy, contacting executive search firms may lead to residual benefits. Although some of the larger search firms may get hundreds of unsolicited resumes a week, the advent of computerized data entry and retrieval has permitted candidate credential retention at volumes far greater than in the old, strictly "hard copy" days. It's not unusual for a recruiter with a well-organized system to initiate contact with a candidate months, or even years, after the initial mailing.
- *Validation*—Passing the recruiter's screening process, and being presented on the slate of proposed candidates, permits you to compete on "a level playing field" with your opponents. Also, chances are that you can avoid— or at least have minimal contact with—the firm's human resources department, an organization typically better at screening out candidates than screening them in.

Disadvantages

- *Timing*—If a recruiter isn't currently working on a search assignment compatible with your background, objectives, salary level, or even location when you're actively seeking a new position, there is no match. Unfortunately, this probability is extremely high at the time of your particular mailing. Somewhere, of course, an executive search firm probably is conducting an assignment matching your career objective and skills. But which one? The remedy is to contact as many search firms as possible.
- *Pain in the Butt Stuff*—Usually, a carefully crafted letter and professionally prepared resume are expected to generate one of three responses from a recruiter. First, a telephone call (the ideal) suggesting that ". . . your credentials appear to be an excellent match with a current assignment. Let's meet." Second, a polite acknowledgement letter and third, no response.

   Here are two other response derivatives which, if occurring with any frequency, will test your patience:

   Sourcing—The recruiter calls, and after your heart skips a beat or two in anticipation, you learn the purpose of the contact is for the recruiter to tap into your network of business associates to fill a search for which you're not qualified.

The best response is to be cooperative. Even though your immediate interests as a potential candidate are not being served, you may be in a position to help both the recruiter and a colleague who, even if not actively searching, may find an excellent new career position through your unselfish efforts. The recruiter will remember, too. And the next time, it may be your turn.

Forms—Very few retainer firms, but approximately 5-10 percent of the contingency firms, will reply to your cover letter/resume by mailing back to you their "form." The implication is that, if the potential candidate devotes the necessary time and effort to complete the form (between 30 and 90 minutes, depending on length) the search firm will be in a better position to help place the candidate as an appropriate client search assignment materializes. If the form is simple and short (seldom the case), fine . . . go ahead and fill it out. After receiving your dozenth form over a two-month period, however, you'll probably change your mind. And, why not? The probability of a "fill out my form first" search firm submitting you as a candidate is no greater than that of a recruiter not wasting your time with administrative nonsense.

2. NETWORK

The purpose of networking is to tap into the people you know, asking them to either make you aware of available positions consistent with your professional objective and background, or to introduce you to their contacts who may be in a similar position to advance your search and, eventually, placement. This strategy takes the old saying "It's not what you know, it's who you know" one step further: "It's not just who you know, it's who you know who knows whom you should get to know."

Networking can serve one of two basic purposes, and the second purpose sometimes has a hidden agenda: a) to gather information about a function or industry you're not familiar with, to help you to determine the feasibility of making such a switch, and b) to plug into a position, probably unadvertised, for which you are qualified.

The "hidden agenda" may come into play here. Remember that networking isn't interviewing. The premise for the network meeting is normally to obtain advice and direction from the contact agreeing to meet with you in the first place so an opening line such as, "I'd like to work with your firm. When can we meet?" isn't likely to be received favorably. Still, it's realistic to expect that, sooner or later, networking will result in your meeting with a decision-maker, in an excellent firm, with whom develops that highly desirable quality of "personal chemistry." Your hidden agenda, then, is to sell yourself as if you were actually being interviewed . . . understanding, of course, that your contact must initiate the first step of soliciting your candidacy with the firm.

The fundamental theory of networking is to request your contact to provide you the names of two to three contacts with whom you may also meet to discuss your career aspirations. If successful, the networking campaign progresses geometrically and, ideally, only ends upon completing the search for a new position.

Advantages

- *Differentiation*—The best cover letter and resume can't sell you like you can sell yourself. Networking is the only strategy of the four that, from the start, permits eye-to-eye contact.
- *Creativity*—A properly managed meeting, and the give-and-take dialogue that ensues, can easily spawn creative ideas on the part of your contact that wouldn't materialize from only a 30-second reading of your resume.
- *No competition*—You're not just one of a dozen candidates being interviewed for the same position this week.

Disadvantages

- *Timing*—The probability of scheduling a meeting is governed by the vagaries of ongoing business and personal commitments, so you must balance perseverance with good judgment.
- *Concentric, Weakening Circles*—Normally, you'll make the biggest "splash" with those who are closest, e.g., family, friends, acquaintances and personal business contacts. The further you extend beyond your inner circle, the less likely you are to be met with meaningful help.
- *Time Consumptive*—Be prepared to spend a lot of time networking if that's your strategy of choice, because it *will* chew up this valuable resource. Unless you're within walking distance to a network contact, or at least a short drive, figure that the combination of a one-hour meeting and round-trip commuting can take as much as a half-day.

3. CONTACT TARGET FIRMS

No matter how extensive your list of personal contacts, or how adept you become at networking, you simply won't be able to meet decision-makers at every firm you find appealing. The next best alternative? Write directly to the firms, sending a one-page cover letter and your resume. Be sure to say why you're leaving (keep it positive) and outline your career objectives. Other important elements:

- *Value Statement*—Although a well-prepared resume outlines responsibilities and accomplishments, a one-paragraph synopsis of your value to the prospective employer in the cover letter serves as a "grabber." After all, the foremost question in the prospective employer's mind is "What can this person do for me?" If the cover letter doesn't stimulate adequate interest, the resume may never get read.

- *Compensation*—Salary, bonus, and "soft dollar" compensation (e.g., deferred, 401(k), stock options, etc.) don't all have to be mentioned in the cover letter. Simply stating your compensation range over the last several years, however, gives the reader insight into your affordability. Omitting this information, however, risks their assuming your financial profile is out of sync with their structure.
- *Call for Action*—Put the ball in their court by asking them to contact you (the soft sell), or risk being called pushy (not all bad) by saying you'll be calling soon for an appointment.

Advantages

- *Differentiation*—As with networking, writing to target firms enables you to present your unique credentials to the decision-maker of your choice . . . assuming your contact actually reads the cover letter/resume. Most do.
- *No Competition*—While any given target firm, at any given time, probably isn't in a position to hire you, you're not competing with others. The advantage is getting your foot in the door before a recruiter is given a search assignment or before the firm decides to run a position available ad in a newspaper.
- *Selectivity*—You can write to whomever you choose and at any time. If the initial mailing is rejected or unanswered, the option is always open to contact the same individual at a later date or, if appropriate, another decision-maker.

Disadvantages

- *Not Read*—There is no guarantee your recipient will actually read your letter and resume—and there are no absolute antidotes for this problem—but two tactics can minimize your being ignored.

    First, you always have the option of making a follow-up phone call within 30 days of the mailing.

    Second, writing to executives just below the top echelon, i.e., those who don't appear on every mailing list, may get attention simply because their in-baskets aren't as filled as those of the target firm's chairman, president, and C.F.O.
- *Timing/Volume*—There is no way to anticipate which target firms may have a need for your services as you undertake a mailing campaign, so the remedy is to generate volume. Target firm letters result in interviews less than five percent of the time and, unless your function is in high demand . . . and unless your credentials and accomplishments are impeccable . . . and, and, and . . . the number is closer to one-two percent.

Getting an interview is not the same as getting a job offer. Figure that, at least, approximately 6-10 interviews are necessary to generate one or two offers.

All these numbers suggest it will take a target firm letter campaign of about 1,000 to materialize in only a few offers, and that's if you stay in your career field. If a career field switch is attempted, plan on boosting the number of letters to 2,000-3,000.

- *Shelf Life*—Target firm letters customarily have a very short shelf life. Either your recipient is interested or not.

- *Geography*—Overcoming the timing problem is hard enough to do without superimposing the geographical barrier, but there are two ways to minimize this difficulty. First, focus out-of-town target firm letters on your current employer's direct competitors, those organizations which presumably would have the most interest in your specific industry experience. Second, assuming you want to relocate to a specific city, evaluate whether your interest is strong enough to warrant your paying the associated travel expenses.

4. REPLY TO POSITION LISTINGS

Position listings tend to be discounted, as if answering an ad is an admission we're looking for a new job (which we are) or replying to an ad is beneath our dignity (which it's not). If those two psychological barriers can be surpassed, the third bias, "It doesn't work," is a favorite of many, and is equally invalid. The fact is, position listings do work. Admittedly, this fourth major strategy may not be as sophisticated, market research-oriented or "refined" as the other three, but its unsexy nature shouldn't disguise the probability that, comparing effort expended vs. results, answering ads holds its own.

Three primary sources to consult for position listings:

- *The Wall Street Journal*—especially Tuesdays. If you're interested in nationwide listings, the *WSJ* also publishes aggregated positions available in its *National Business Employment Weekly*.

- *Local Newspapers*—Particularly in large metropolitan areas, position listings appear daily. Sunday editions usually feature the largest number of these advertisements.

- *Other*—Certain professional and trade organizations, as well as some colleges/universities, publish position listings in periodic magazines and newsletters. Not all do, of course, but it's worth investigating.

Advantages

- *Easy*—An ad response is relatively easy and doesn't absorb a lot of time.
- *Timing/Defined Need*—By its very placement, a position listing announces a defined staffing need, and a need now. No mass mailings to target firms

or executive recruiters here. No time-consuming hours in arranging and meeting network contacts either. If you believe a "fit" exists, a single mail piece and a trip to the nearest mailbox is all it takes.

Disadvantages

- *Competition*—Face it. This strategy screams for competition. But if your functional qualifications, industry experience and salary are compatible with the specifications presented in the ad, you may find the competition isn't so stiff after all.
- *Singular Transaction*—Of the four major search strategies, responding to a position listing typically has the shortest shelf life. In fact, it's probably fair to say there is no shelf life: your reply is either classified a "go" or "no go."

There is no magic formula for changing employers effectively. But, pursuing each of the four major career search strategies, combined with persevering hard work, luck, and faith, will make the process less imperfect.

Mr. Mohar is a management consultant from Naperville, Illinois, specializing in strategy implementation. He is a former job search candidate and wrote this article from his own experience.

A Basic Approach to Job Changing

Twelve steps to guide you from self-appraisal to negotiating offers

by William E. Gould

Statistics indicate that executives typically change jobs five to six times in their business lives. There are many reasons to change, ranging from the need to generate more income to the avoidance of career plateauing and burnout. Whatever the reason, the following is a basic 12-step plan for changing jobs that will help you maximize opportunities while minimizing risks.

Step 1: Do a thorough self-appraisal. It is essential to find out everything about that itch that says, "I've got to look around." To determine what's bothering you, analyze your job, yourself and your needs. Questions to consider are: What do I like about my current job? What don't I like about it? What is the culture of my current environment?

In addition, you should ask: What is my personality? How do others perceive me? Is my style autocratic or participative? What are the characteristics of a "perfect environment" for me?

And finally, you must say: What kind of community do I want to live in? What schools, recreation, and social life must be a part of that community? What is my and my family's tolerance for travel? Do I want to commute to my job? If so, how long and by what mode?

Step 2: Analyze the effects of a job change on your spouse, your children and yourself. It is essential to share your thoughts with your family. Handled improperly, you can become an unpopular person in the household at a time when you need complete family support.

If your spouse is working and you change cities, will your spouse be able to find a new job? Or, if your spouse stops working, can you stand the loss of one income while one of you conducts a job search?

How will relocating affect your children? If they are in high school, will your daughter, who is just becoming her own person, be able to handle a move? Is your son going to land that quarterback position in a new school?

And finally, are you psychologically prepared to pull up old and trusted roots, move to a new company and start all over again as a new person on the block?

Step 3: Prepare a resume.   There are hundreds of formats to choose from. The key to resume writing is to give the reader a brief outline of your business life and education without telling your life story. Save the details for the personal interview.

Don't include your job objective. A cover letter tailored to a particular job or company should mention your objective. Remember, everything you send out gives a signal about you. Invest in quality paper and typesetting. Make it look like an executive resume.

Step 4: Prepare a target list of companies that best suits your needs.   Researching companies takes time and you will find it difficult to fit this into your everyday schedule. Nevertheless, you must have this list in front of you before talking to anyone.

Step 5: Determine your target acceptance date.   It takes a minimum of three months to conduct a job campaign. Select a date for accepting an offer that is at *least* 12 weeks from the time you begin looking. You need enough time to develop options.

The timing of your search strategy is critical. Corporations tend to hire during two periods: February through June and September through November. Backing up at least three months from the middle of the cycles, the best times to begin the process of changing jobs are in January and July.

If you are pressured to accept an offer before your targeted date, tell the company that you need a certain amount of time to explore opportunities and that you will make your decision by a specific date. Emphasize that you are not out of a job, that this is one of the most important decisions in life and that you want to make the right choice.

Offers typically come 9 to 12 weeks into your search. However, you must discipline yourself not to accept before you have reviewed enough opportunities. In this way, you can be sure to make the right decision.

Step 6: To minimize the risk of exposure within your company,   put the word out among a few trusted friends who may know of opportunities. This is the least risky approach. It will be 8 to 12 weeks before word begins to filter back to your organization. Remember also that this approach is the one least likely to yield that ideal opportunity as the probability of your friends being in a target company is low.

Step 7: Put the word out with executive search consultants. This keeps your risk of exposure to a minimum while expanding your outreach.

In selecting search firms, you can contact the Association of Executive Search Consultants, Inc. in New York, NY, whose member firms subscribe to a professional code of ethics, assuring you of strict confidentiality. In addition, Kennedy Publications in Fitzwilliam, NH, publishes *The Directory of Executive Recruiters*. Either source can provide a comprehensive listing of professional recruiters.

At each firm you contact, request a 15 or 20 minute get-acquainted visit. This meeting puts your face in their file. Don't be offended, however, if the executive search firm will not see you. It just means they probably don't have an assignment that is appropriate to your background. Search firms are busy focusing on their clients' needs and cannot have time to see everyone who contacts them.

Nevertheless, every firm is interested in knowing the availability of good people. So make a follow-up call to reinforce your original contact. The risk of exposure from an executive search firm is low.

Once you begin to meet prospective employers, expect word to get back to your company in four to six weeks. Prepare for the possibility of discovery and immediate dismissal. Remember, it takes longer to find a job without a job, especially if you are more than 50 years old.

Step 8: When your intentions are fully public, pull out the stops. Use your college alumni records and your association membership lists and cross-reference these people with your original target list. Use annual reports, 10K's, every lead you can think of.

The most effective and rewarding way of gaining entry is through a recommendation by someone. Try to find introductions into target companies where you don't have firsthand acquaintances. Call your contact and explain why you would like to be introduced to the firm.

Step 9: When you have an interview at the ideal target company, approach it as a learning experience. It's a chance to learn about yourself, the job opportunity and the person interviewing you.

Get rid of your anger, if you have any. Negative exhortations about your current situation work against you. Let off steam before the interview, and get your defenses under control. Relax, be positive, and be open, honest and candid.

Listen carefully to interviewers. Be open to their sequence of questions and, above all, don't try to control the interview. Your resume answers basic historical questions, but you should expect to answer certain inevitable questions, such as:

what are your strengths and weaknesses and what is your management style? Never attempt to sell an idealized concept of who you should be; sell yourself by being yourself.

Always be candid about your salary, bonus and perks, titles, responsibilities and college degrees. Be truthful, as someone will check this information.

Feel free to go on the offensive and ask the questions you want answered. Why is the position open? What happened in the past in this area? Will you be blocked? Is the boss' temperament a problem?

It is important to ask about company politics. Is the job in the corporate mainstream? Where is it likely to lead? What is the future strategy of the corporation? How will it affect your particular area?

Step 10: After several interviews, rank your options and choose the finalist.   Go back for as many repeat visits as you need to really get to know those companies. Don't hesitate to investigate them thoroughly; they are going to investigate you!

Step 11: Negotiate your terms.   Timing is very important in negotiations. If they conclude too quickly, you probably neglected some issues. On the other hand, if negotiations go on and on, the potential employer may start to cool, and you risk having the offer withdrawn.

Therefore, ask important questions early in the negotiation process to avoid nitpicking in the latter stages; look into: state and local taxes, living costs, mortgage differential (most companies now make up the difference between your existing rate and the new rate on your current base from two to five years) and moving costs.

In addition, learn what pre-tax benefits are available, such as cars (an important perk today that can be worth $8,000 to $10,000 in income), club memberships and medical insurance. Find out about incentive compensation, performance share programs and stock options, and explore profit sharing, pension plans, and of course, your starting salary. Minimum switching premiums today are running between 10% and 20%. Where in the salary range for the position are you? Will you experience salary compression by coming in at the top half of the top quartile with this new company? Investigate bonuses. What is the range? How many years in the past 10 have they been paid out?

Don't overlook vacations. Regardless of stated "policy," if a company wants you badly enough, they often can compromise. It's tough to go backward.

Step 12: When you have negotiated several offers, and your target date has arrived, you have to make a decision.   Listen to your instincts: they are important. Listen to what your family says; their instincts are superb! They know you best and will pick up signals you may not discern. Before making any final decision, look into local living conditions, schools, etc., with your family. Ideally, have an interview dinner on their turf with all other spouses present. They can be revealing. You will learn the company's values and norms.

Your new employer is going to require references. You should be thinking of several past superiors, peers and subordinates who can be contacted. It is in your best interest to delay this until the last possible moment. When someone in your office is called for a reference, your intention to leave the company is completely exposed. During the negotiation stage, have several relatively "safe" references of people who will respect a confidence. Save the last references for the time when you have a firm offer.

Finally, enjoy the rewards that come from the challenges of change.

William E. Gould is managing director of Gould McCoy & Chadick, Inc., a New York-based executive search firm, and was president of the Association of Executive Search Consultants.

When to Make a Career Move: How to Increase Your Marketability

An interview with Barbara L. Provus

by Julie Bain

When should an executive consider making a career change?
There are push and pull factors. Pull factors are magnets, things that would attract you out of what you are doing today to pursue a really great opportunity. Push factors are the things that are nudging at you on a day-to-day basis—frustration with your boss, you don't see promotion opportunities, you're traveling five days a week. If there are enough push factors, I think it's time to at least evaluate your options.

Is long-term loyalty to a company still rewarded?
Careers today tend to be mobile. Ten years ago, companies that were hiring were leery of the executive who had made several moves. Now, 10 years later, we have the opposite. We're leery of individuals who have *never* made a move, because we wonder if perhaps no one saw them as excellent candidates. Plus, they have less variety of experience. Many companies today are looking for hybrids. They want the person who perhaps spent the early years of his or her career with a very respected, well-managed company such as a GE, a Xerox, or an IBM of the old days. But if that person has never had a more hands-on, entrepreneurial, leaner-resources type of experience, that person is not viewed as attractive a candidate as the person who has been with three or four different companies and has gleaned the best practices from each of them.

Are companies laying off their long-term, highly paid, older employees and hiring younger, lower-paid employees?
No, companies today are looking for more experience, and at the higher levels the more senior candidates may actually have an advantage. They may cost a little more, but I think as companies are realizing that they have to do more with less, they may feel the person who has 20 to 25 years of experience can actually bring more to the organization than the person who's only got 10 years. But, again, we're talking about the senior positions. Middle management is the endangered species.

If you feel like you are an endangered species in your company, how can you make yourself indispensable?
Get some additional skills, experience, or exposure. Perhaps you've only been in one product area; maybe you could move into another operating division of your company. International experience is crucial today. Do whatever it takes to gain some responsibility for a global market. And, in spite of everything that's been written lately about the MBA, it is still, in the business world, a valuable degree.

Say you're a 50 year-old, fairly highly placed executive, your company downsizes or is acquired, and all of a sudden you are out of a job. What are the first steps you should take?
The first step is to make sure you are offered outplacement. It's a big mistake to take additional salary or severance in lieu of outplacement. Finding a job will be a full-time job. There are books on the market, but it's not something you want to tackle on your own. If you haven't mailed out at least 500 resumes, you are not doing a thorough job search. It's a direct-mail campaign; you have to cast as wide a net as possible. And don't forget networking. Pull all the cards from your Rolodex that you've collected over the past few years and let those people know you're available. Also, think about the leaders in your field who might recommend you for a position when a recruiter calls them. Let them know you're actively looking for a job.

Do you subscribe to the latest theory espousing long, detailed resumes?
I prefer someone err on the side of length and detail. I certainly don't want the 25-page CV, but a one-page resume doesn't tell me much other than title, company, and date. Three to four pages work best, using chronological order with specific accomplishments and responsibilities, to whom you reported, and your staff size. If you're one of the Fortune 500 companies, then I know something about your business and industry. But if you work for some start-up or some very small privately held company, explain what your company does.

What can a recruiter do for me that I can't do for myself?
We can help you assess opportunities in a more objective manner. If you are employed, when something comes to your attention, you have to decide whether you are interested or not. If you're interested, you pursue it; if you're not, then you wait for the next opportunity to present itself. A recruiter can help you with your long-term career goals.

A recruiter also offers you confidentiality. Often it's important that you are not directly approached by a company because your first reaction, in order to protect your current situation, is to say, "Thank you, I'm not interested. I'm happy where I am." But if recruiters call you, you'll probably be more comfortable talking to them because you know they are not going to share your background with their clients or with other companies without your knowledge and permission. And they will also put you in the database for future reference. You may have a lot of contacts, but you can't possibly know every opportunity that's out there. We may call you back six or 12 months later with something that really is a good fit for you that you never would have been able to find without the help of a recruiter. And then finally, if you do go through the assessment process, are on the candidate slate, and ultimately receive the offer, the recruiter will, in effect, act as your agent. It's a lot easier to negotiate a compensation package if there's a go-between.

How much does compensation motivate executive career moves?
Money is not the major factor. Of course, no one really wants to take a step down. But today people are attracted to the opportunity to have an impact on the organization. It may be a longer-term payoff, meaning equity or significant stock options in a company. Or it may just be the chance to have fun again. I have had some very senior executives say that for the last chapter of their careers, they wouldn't mind going back a few steps, because they would like to have one last fun job before they retire.

Are people honest about their current compensation with you? It seems that's one area where people would be tempted to fudge.
I encourage people always to be honest with an executive recruiter. We will sometimes ask for verification from the W-2 form. Also, when I'm doing the final reference, which is usually with the individual's most recent boss, I will ask the individual's compensation. And of course, if you're with a public company and you're one of the top-paid executives, it is public record anyway. If you inflate your salary early on, it could backfire. There could be other candidates who are making less money and who therefore might be a little more attractive to the client. The fact that you inflated your salary by 10 or 15 percent could eliminate you as a candidate. The big increases that people used to associate with changing companies are no longer there; it used to be the norm to expect a 20 to 25 percent

increase when changing companies; now 10 to 15 percent would be quite generous.

Candidates may also be tempted to say, "What I'm making now is not relevant."
I will not pursue someone who will not tell me. And yet on the converse, I feel it's only fair to the candidate to know what my client is paying in terms of the base and a bonus. Often there could be flexibility, but I want the candidate to know up front how close or far apart we are.

How do you find employee candidates?
First we target with our client where this person might be, what kind of industry background we want the candidate to have, and, many times, specific companies. Sometimes companies want to recruit directly from their own industry, so the person will come in with knowledge of that industry. Other times they will want to go to a completely different industry for a new viewpoint and perspective. Then our director of research uses books and directories to try to identify individuals within those industries and companies who, at least by virtue of their title, might be potential candidates or sources of candidates. We also maintain a database of candidates from previous searches, which at this point is up to about 3,000 to 4,000 people.

Do you prefer employed candidates?
Ten years ago I would ask the question: "Will you consider candidates who are unemployed?" Clients would say, "I don't want to see anyone who is unemployed." A couple of years later, they would think for a minute and then say, "Well, I guess so, if they're unemployed for the right reasons—an acquisition, or the company was divested. But they'd have to be *really* good." The next stage was, "You know, you might be able to find some candidates who are unemployed and really a little more qualified than we need. But perhaps because they're unemployed they'd be willing to look at this opportunity." So it was almost a plus. And now, I have *clients* who got to their present positions after being unemployed. They understand. The stigma is not there as much.

How do you evaluate and measure potential candidates?
The first evaluation is: Does that person's work experience match what my client is seeking from a technical or functional perspective? We're forgetting the individuals at this point; we are truly just looking at the industries they have been with, the companies they've been with, the positions they've held, the management and budget responsibilities they've had, and results or accomplishments in those jobs. This is primarily a paper evaluation—looking at a resume.

Then you get into the issue of assessment, and it's important to know not only what your clients say they want, but you have to pick up nuances. Most clients today are seeking someone who can have an impact on their organization, who is going to be worth more to that company than the previous person who was in that position, or is going to be some sort of catalyst. You have to assess your client's culture to see what kind of person, what kind of approach, what kind of interpersonal style, even what kind of image is going to fit best. That person has to have technical and personal credibility and be able to establish rapport throughout the organization.

Have you recruited many women to top-level positions?
Ten years ago clients would say, "No, I don't think a woman would be a good candidate because the corporate culture wouldn't accept her or a minority." And, although that may have been the case, they certainly didn't want to be proactive about changing that culture. Then it was, "Gee, if you could find a *qualified* female or minority, yes, I would consider them." So it was still not a very aggressive stance. Now it is almost expected that there will be women and, hopefully, minorities on any candidate slate.

Barbara L. Provus is founder and principal in the Chicago firm of
Shepherd, Bueschel & Provus, Inc.
Julie Bain is editor in chief of Private Clubs *magazine.*

Strategies to Ease a Career Transition

Avoid the negativism that can lead to disaster

by Stanlee Phelps

Nervous or uncertain about what to do now that you're unemployed? Angry at your former boss, company or yourself for allowing this to happen? Too embarrassed to face your friends?

Relax. Such feelings are normal for anyone who's just suffered a job loss. Even the calmest people are likely to experience dread, panic, shame or sadness. Instead of assuming you've gone haywire, consider yours to be a typical reaction and take steps to minimize your discomfort so you can begin a productive job search.

Here are 15 tips to help you make a smoother transition into your job hunt:

1. **Don't panic.** As difficult as it is to believe right now, your life is changing, not ending. Now is your opportunity to create a new and highly satisfying work situation.

2. **Don't blow up in public.** You may be tempted to "tell people off" at your former employer, or take the opportunity to settle old scores. Don't make the mistake of burning your bridges behind you. Expressing angry feelings is healthy, but be selective about how, when, where and with whom it's done.

3. **Don't fault yourself.** Blaming yourself will keep you focused on the past rather than the future. Learn from your mistakes, but don't make yourself miserable.

4. **Don't criticize your former boss or the company to anyone, particularly prospective employers.** This will always work against you, since it raises questions about how well (or poorly) you deal with difficult situations. It's also likely to

create a negative impression of *you,* rather than the company. At the very least, it'll suggest you're likely to be as critical of your new employer as you are of your old one.

5. **Be cooperative if your duties are being transferred.** Keep up the quality of your work and be willing to train any replacement. Though it may be difficult, it's wiser to support the company in its planned changes than interfere with them. It's unreasonable to expect the company to support you in your re-employment efforts if you don't support its efforts to proceed with its operations.

6. **Avoid social or emotional isolation.** Many other managers have preceded you into the job search. Contact people you know who've been in similar circumstances. If they seem open, share your feelings and ask how they worked through theirs.

    One displaced executive discovered through his wife that four of his neighbors were also in transition. Instead of hiding out, the couple invited the neighbors, along with their spouses, over for coffee. They eventually formed a support group and met regularly at cookouts to share ideas, feelings and networking contacts.

7. **Don't try to keep your termination a secret.** You won't be able to anyway. The more secretive you are, the harder it'll be for others to help you. One unemployed man told his wife not to tell anyone of his job loss and shut himself off from the support and contacts he needed. A month after a counselor persuaded him to open up, he secured a position by networking, rather than from mailings or ads, which he originally believed would work magic.

8. **Don't avoid your close friends, but be prepared to have some so-called friends disappoint you.** Understand and accept that your circumstances may make some people uncomfortable. Folks whom you thought were friends will drift away. It may be because you're no longer in a position to help them, but it's more likely they identify with your difficulty and feel unable to help. Don't let their irrationality upset you. It really says more about them than about you.

9. **Avoid the temptation to immediately tell all your professional colleagues about your situation.** These people might be key sources of job leads, but if you contact them prematurely, you may present a scattered or unprofessional picture. Formulate clear career objectives and have your emotions well under control before contacting business associates for job search purposes.

10. **Discuss your situation with your family.** They all have a stake in it and have feelings that should be aired. Children, especially young ones, may have irrational fears that need to be allayed. For instance it's not uncommon for them to wonder, "Do we all have to go to jail now?" Give

everyone the opportunity to express their feelings, then be supportive, while allowing them to support you.

11. **Make your search a full-time job.** Prepare to spend at least 40 hours a week job hunting. There are enough job search strategies and activities to easily fill several full-time work weeks. Set up a daily schedule and stick to it. Dress for the office, not for yard work. Establish a routine that's comfortable and productive. It's critical that others believe you're serious about finding a job.

Never advertise when you're taking a day to play hookey. For instance, don't leave a message saying that you've gone to the beach on your answering machine during office hours. "You can't believe how frequently I find out that someone is out playing for the day," says one human resources manager. While playing is essential to a healthy transition, it's wise to do so discreetly, especially when you want to be viewed as ready to go back to work.

12. **Be prepared for rejection.** Maintaining a positive yet realistic attitude will help reduce feelings of disappointment if job offers are slow to develop. Remember that you're looking for the right position, not just any position. Therefore, consider a negative response from a prospective employer as simply an opportunity to investigate other leads with greater potential.

13. **Don't expect your campaign to be successful overnight.** It can take several months to locate the satisfying and rewarding position you seek. Be patient. In hindsight, you'll likely decide the search was as enriching as the position to which it led.

One executive humorously recalls spending three months intensively interviewing and preparing a proposal for a potential employer. When he didn't hear back from the company and his phone calls weren't returned, he became worried. He finally found out the owners had been arrested and jailed when the Federal Bureau of Investigation showed up at his front door inquiring about his connection to the two men.

14. **Keep your sense of humor and relax.** Recognize that any disaster you experience during your search has already befallen other job seekers. For example, one eager candidate was so anxious about an interview that he tripped over the carpeting and fell down in front of the receptionist's desk. Nervous about the memorable first impression he'd made thus far, he proceeded to knock a few items off the interviewer's desk. Today, he considers it one of his funniest stories.

15. **Be kind to yourself.** Reward yourself a little more after a trying stint of job hunting. Give yourself permission to do some pleasurable things you've been postponing: Visit the beach, zoo or museum; read a good

book; go to the theater, or see old friends. Take more time to be with the people who support and nurture you.

Stanlee Phelps is a vice president in the Irvine, Calif., office of Lee Hecht Harrison Inc., a New York-based outplacement firm.

How to Resign Smoothly and Amicably

by Frederick Hornberger

Once you've nailed down your new job—and not before, if at all possible—comes time to tie things off at your current employer.

(Incidentally, don't fall for the "wisdom" of resigning to devote full-time to your job search. Neither should you indulge yourself by quitting in a huff, despite the temptation. No matter what they say, potential employers—and the recruiters who represent them—view unemployment as a condition that demands an explanation, though in these days of massive downsizing the explanation can be quite plausible.)

Resigning—like firing—is never easy, especially when you've worked at a position for several years, and have become part of a team. Some employers and co-workers take it personally and accuse you of abandoning ship. However, the following precautions can make your resignation relatively smooth and amicable.

Make Up Your Mind

Before you submit your resignation, you must be clearly committed to leaving.

Have you already pursued all avenues for advancement within your firm? Before accepting another job, give your present job a fair chance. Visit with your boss and other key personnel to learn where your career stands and what plans are in place for you. Give your firm every consideration. This will help you commit to your new opportunity once you decide to leave.

Keep Resignations Short, Simple and Positive

Leave your employer on a positive note. Your moving on does not have to be a time for long faces. After all, you have just won an opportunity to advance, an opportunity for which you owe your employer sincere thanks. Thank your colleagues, too, for their help in preparing you to move onward and upward. Naturally, you will be missed if you have given your best to the job you are leaving—and you will be especially missed by those inconvenienced by your leaving! Let them know that you intend to assist them in whatever ways you can. By showing your boss and firm due respect, you encourage future support you may need someday.

Keep conversation simple and concise when you resign. The more you say, the more questions you may have to answer. Avoid lengthy discussion with your old employer about your new opportunity. Because your boss is losing a valued employee, he or she may express negative opinions about your new firm or position which will only confuse you. You may find yourself having to justify your personal goals and decisions, or absorb personal frustration. If you're dealing with volatile or vindictive personalities, it may be best to avoid telling anyone where you will be going.

Typically, your resignation means a lot of work for your old employer. Someone will be left with the burden of replacing you and dealing with the loss of department productivity due to your vacancy. Chances are your boss will be caught off guard with your resignation, and will not be able to listen clearly to your explanations anyway because of concerns with the department's new predicament. One can never gauge the reaction of a boss when a key employee resigns, but it is always to your advantage to keep the atmosphere positive and supportive.

If you feel you may end up having to function in an uncooperative atmosphere, you may want to resign right after your work day so that you are no longer on company time and in control of your own. If you must have a discussion with your employer, try to schedule it for the following morning when everyone can have the opportunity to face the situation objectively. If during the meeting you are having to defend yourself, or if things begin to get out of control, motion for another meeting at a more appropriate time.

The Oral Resignation

This is usually the more difficult type of resignation because it may place you in the compromising position of having to explain your good decision. Words are very powerful, and are particularly charged during this time. Be careful what you say. It is common for your old boss to probe you for information that may have led up to your decision. Bosses often want to know who or what is the reason for your leaving, or if you have any suggestions to offer which can help make the organization more effective. If you have had a close relationship with your boss, you may feel obligated to share your heart in confidence.

Don't fall for this trap! Use your head and discuss personal and heartfelt matters outside the office. Remember this boss is still your boss. Whatever you say will be viewed as biased, and may eventually be used against you. At this point you are no longer considered a team player, nor are you considered to have the company's best interest at heart. Too often individuals get hurt by comments that are either misinterpreted, or exaggerated. Constructive criticism is no longer your responsibility, and carries with it a high cost that could affect your good references.

It is always best instead to sing the praises of the firm and those you worked with. Determine beforehand several positive aspects of your workplace, and mention them liberally (even if they were only the great lunches and humorous stories told over coffee). You want to be perceived as someone who was positive and moving forward with your old job. People will remember you best by your last impression. Make it your best performance.

The Written Resignation

The easiest resignation is a written one where you have time to effectively prepare what you wish to communicate. A written resignation reinforces the fact that you are really leaving and not simply threatening in order to renegotiate your position. Also, there is something permanent about the written word which often circumvents interrogation.

Under no circumstance should you state any dissatisfactions with the firm or individuals. Not only is it good manners to stress the positive when leaving, but what you put down will remain in your file long after individuals and circumstances that may have caused you dissatisfaction are gone. You never know when your future paths may cross again.

Remember to keep things short, simple and positive.

The Counteroffer

Surveys show that eight out of ten employees who accept counteroffers don't complete the following year with their employer.[1]

Why shun counteroffers? Because the factors that caused you to consider an outside move generally remain in force. Besides, your current employer may lose trust in your loyalty. Accepting a counteroffer may permanently damage your reputation with your would-be-employer. It may conclude that you were merely using them to gain leverage—you weren't in earnest as a candidate. Never underestimate the value of your perceived integrity in this situation.

The best response to a counteroffer is to listen politely, perhaps even sleep on it, but decline. If your current firm denied you advancement before you secured an outside offer, it will probably thwart you next time you feel ready to advance.

1. Hawkinson, Paul. "Counteroffer Acceptance, the Road to Career Ruin." *National Business Employment Weekly.* Dec. 11, 1983.

What's more, your firm may start looking to replace you the day you accept the counteroffer. Your plans for leaving may not be forgotten!

Leave on the Right Note

Before leaving the firm, take time to speak with each of your support staff, peers, executive personnel, and others with whom you've worked. Clear up any unsettled business with people and projects. Be sensitive to their reactions and keep your conversations positive and constructive. Some people may naturally express their own discontent and may egg you on to agree with them. Don't. Instead, express your appreciation and tell your colleagues you'll miss them. A little time spent nurturing relationships before leaving for your new job will go a long way to build support for your future.

Also keep in mind that it is professional courtesy to give your employer ample time to transition you out of the firm, typically two to four weeks. However, you should try to get out as soon as possible to avoid recurring attempts by others for you to tell your story, and to avoid having to deal with the frustrations and pressures at the job as the firm adjusts to your leaving.

Frederick Hornberger, CPC, is president of Hornberger Management Company, a Wilmington, Delaware-based executive search firm.

Understanding Executive Search: A Candidate's Perspective

by J. Larry Tyler

Executive search firms are growing and becoming increasingly involved in the process of hiring executives. As a potential candidate, you need to learn some of the new rules for dealing with these firms. If you can appreciate the differences between firms, you'll operate with more realistic expectations and gain more control over the hiring process.

Executive search firms developed after World War II when an expanding economy caused shortages of skilled labor. A "middle man" was needed to facilitate employment. In many of these early agencies, the applicant paid the employment fee (*Applicant Paid Fee* or *APF*). Today, APF firms are unheard of in healthcare and viewed as an anachronism in the search business.

From APFs there sprang up a new kind of agency. In contingency search, the employer paid the fee, but only if a hire was made. The fee was therefore "contingent" upon placement of a candidate. At about the same time, another fee arrangement evolved. Focusing on the senior executive level, these agencies took a consulting approach to employment. An executive search firm was engaged exclusively to seek candidates for an employer and a fee was paid during the course of the search. In other words, these firms were "retained," giving birth to the term, "retained search."

In today's environment, there are both contingency and retained firms. On a dollar volume basis, they divide up the employment market fairly equally. But while the results of contingency and retained search are the same (someone gets hired), their approaches are different. Because these firms vary in both approach and payment, you'll need to adjust your expectations and how you deal with them. *Figure 1* notes some of the major differences.

40

40

Figure 1

RETAINER	CONTINGENCY
■ Fee paid by employer during the search regardless of results	■ Fee contingent on placement
■ Exclusive assignment with client	■ Probably not exclusive
■ Out-of-pocket expenses paid by client to search firm	■ No out-of-pocket expenses paid
■ Survey visit to client	■ No survey visit
■ Contract	■ Contingency contract
■ Salary ranges 50K +	■ 20-100K salary range, but may go higher
■ Not in business to get you a job	■ Wants to get you hired
■ Provides comprehensive report on candidate: resume, references, interview	■ Often forwards resume and brief references only
■ Limited number of opportunities offered to a candidate	■ Exposure to many opportunities
■ Confidentiality generally assumed	■ Confidentiality could be at risk
■ Presents 3 to 5 candidates on average	■ Sends numerous candidates
■ May present you to only one client at a time	■ Will freely circulate your resume
■ Smooth closing negotiations and one-year guarantee over fee payment	■ Potential conflicts between firms or firms and clients

Retainer Firms

Your primary advantages in working with a retained firm are:

- Exclusivity on a job opportunity.
- A thorough selection process.
- Full information on the work setting.
- Protected confidentiality.

The process begins when the search consultant visits the client's organization for a site survey. In this phase, the consultant interviews executives to develop a candidate profile and secures information for prospective candidates such as community background, annual reports and job descriptions. In addition, the consultant establishes a compensation range for the position, plans the search schedule, sets target dates, and most important, gains a sense of the organization's dynamics and management style. It's easy to see why employers who enter into this exhaustive process are usually serious about filling a position.

Recruitment begins with networks in the profession. Consultants identify candidates from target organizations and professional groups such as the American College of Healthcare Executives, state hospital associations and graduate programs in health services administration. Through advertising and direct mail, consultants seek out executives to participate in the process or to offer referrals to other executives.

When you receive a call from a retained search consultant, expect to hear a brief description about the opportunity as well as specifications for the candidate such as years of experience, educational qualifications and specific technical skills. If there's a strong match between the opportunity and your background, the consultant will request your resume and then check references and verify degrees and certifications.

If you seem like an exceptionally good fit, the consultant will arrange to interview you in more depth. Be aware that during this initial screening process, the consultant is trying to produce three to five candidates who meet the client's needs. Expect to receive regular feedback on your standing in the search process, but be assertive about asking questions and be generous in supplying information about yourself, including your special needs for making a move.

If you change your mind about the position, extend the courtesy of dropping out early. It's best for everyone involved: you, the client, the consultant and the other candidates. If you wait until the last minute to drop out, you may not get a second chance.

About six to eight weeks into the engagement, the consultant will send candidate reports of the finalists to the client, including references and interview notes. The client will then decide to interview the finalists or request additional candidates from the consultant.

The retained search approach offers several advantages:

1. Before meeting the client personally, you're introduced through a comprehensive and objective package. Your candidacy is given a fair chance, and even if the client decides on someone else, the consultant offers you feedback that's useful for future interviews.

2. If you're selected to interview with the client, the search consultant sticks with you through the process of first and second interviews, community tours and compensation negotiations.

3. If you're hired, a retained search firm also offers a one-year guarantee on your success. In other words, if you leave or are terminated within a year, the search firm will conduct another search at no charge. However cynical

that may seem, it adds a boost to your move because the client is assured of satisfaction.

4. Through retained search, you received an expert recommendation for a high-level position, but preclude the chance of being presented for several positions at once or having a recruiter "campaign" for you.

It's best to work with a number of retained search firms, keeping your file updated and establishing contacts over time. But be sure to be as selective as the firms are and narrow down your choices of positions, locations and compensation. The consultant will wonder if you appear too eager for too many types of positions. Even if you're not actively looking and just want to stay abreast of the career market and keep your options open, relationships with several retained search firms are a good idea.

When you send your resume to a retained search firm, you'll usually receive some sort of acknowledgement. If the organization has more than one office, be sure to send a copy to the head of each office. Once you make the initial contact, it may be some time before you receive a response, but don't get discouraged. Remember that retainer firms work on fewer searches so your activity with any one firm may be limited. However, when activity does occur, it will usually be meaningful and substantial.

Contingency Firms

Contingency firms can give you lots of exposure and their approach usually works well for junior, middle and unemployed executives. If you're in senior management, the method can still work if the listing is legitimate and if it offers an excellent opportunity with an organization you wouldn't otherwise have contacted. Contingency firms sometimes have "exclusives" with a client, but more often they don't. So be careful about offering them permission to use your resume.

Contingency search differs from retained search because contingency firms don't have contracts or expenses paid by the client. Site surveys, extensive candidate screening and follow-through are impossible under this system. Of course, this doesn't mean that the process is any less effective; it's just different.

If you get a call from a contingency recruiter, you can expect a brief description of the opportunity but usually no exact identification of the position. This is because the contingency recruiter has to protect the listing from candidates who may try to go directly to the employer or from having the opening fed to other agencies.

Once the contingency recruiter has your resume, you'll hear as much information as possible under the circumstances. But you'll probably need to look out for yourself in researching the employer and evaluating whether your qualifications fit the opportunity. The contingency recruiter typically guarantees candidates for only 90 days, so there's a tendency to take a chance and send your resume out to many employers.

If you're local, the recruiter may want to help market your candidacy. Although you might be offered numerous interviews, take care to invest your time only in strong opportunities. Contingency recruiters are enthusiastic advocates and often their motto is, "When in doubt, send em out!" It's up to you to look after your interests and avoid being cajoled into a string of dead-end meetings.

If you find a listing that interests you, keep in mind that you may be on your own during the interviewing process and in final negotiations. It will be far more challenging to feel at ease with your potential employer than if you were working through retained search.

The best way to qualify a recruiter is to ask these questions:

1. Do you have an exclusive?
2. Can you reveal the full information on the client?
3. Will I be notified before my resume is sent to your client?
4. Do you operate on a contingency fee or retainer basis?
5. What is your screening process—interviews, references, etc.?

Asking these questions will help you determine what kind of recruiter you're dealing with. At that point, you can tailor your expectations and act accordingly.

Healthcare executives can easily confuse executive search firms with outplacement/career counseling firms. Outplacement firms are in business to coach you on getting a job. Although they don't guarantee job placement, these firms have an important role in the job search process. For a fee that's typically 15 percent of your compensation, they help you develop a resume, practice interviewing on videotape, identify career goals through vocational testing and build a network of contacts. If you haven't been in the job market for many years or if you left your last employer under traumatic circumstances, you might be a good candidate for outplacement counseling.

Your first and best line of action in career development is your own network. The majority of positions are still filled through personal contacts well before any search firm has made a proposal. You don't necessarily need representation or advocacy from search firms. A high profile in the profession, a strong track record of accomplishments and an extensive network of industry contacts will make you desirable and accessible to employers and search firms. Rest assured: Your head will be hunted. Just keep in mind that search firms augment your own efforts; they don't replace them.

If you haven't been exposed to executive search firms and don't know where to seek them out, you might want to take a look at the classified sections of trade publications. Another excellent source is *The Directory of Executive Recruiters* from Kennedy Publications.

J. Larry Tyler is president of Tyler & Company in Atlanta, Georgia, a firm offering executive search, physician search and human resources consulting. Mr. Tyler is a member of the American College of Healthcare Executives and a credentialed member of the American Association of Healthcare Consultants.

Pros and Cons of Contacting Executive Search Firms

by Richard Nelson Bolles

When other types of agencies don't pay off, every job-hunter pricks up his or her ears upon hearing that there are actually firms which are retained by employers to find people for them. *Naturally,* these agencies/firms/organizations know about vacancies. They're being paid to *fill* them! Incidentally, the very existence of this thriving industry testifies to the fact that employers are as baffled by our country's Neanderthal job-hunting "system" as we are. **Employers don't know how to find decent employees, any more than job-hunters know how to find decent employers.**

Small problem: are these firms looking for unemployed job-hunters? No, no, no. Unhappily (from the job-hunter's point of view) the mission these firms have been given by employers is *to hire away from other firms or employers,* workers who are already employed, and rising—executives, salespeople, technicians, or whatever. *(In the old days, these firms searched only for executives, hence their now-outdated title.)*

Well, let's do our usual rundown:

Names: Executive search firms, executive recruiters, executive recruitment consultants, executive development specialists, management consultants, recruiters.

Nicknames: Headhunters, body snatchers, flesh peddlers, talent scouts.

Number: More than 2,000 firms, with over 12,000 employees.

Volume of business: They have combined billings of more than two and a half billion dollars a year.

Number of vacancies handled by a firm: As a rule, each staff member can only handle 6 to 8 searches at a time;

so, multiply number of staff that a firm has (if known) times 6. Majority of firms have 1 to 2 staff (hence, are handling 6 to 12 current openings); a few have 4 to 5 staff (24 to 30 openings are being searched for); and the largest have staffs handling 80 to 100 openings.

Not surprisingly, there are places that will sell you lists of such firms, for example:

1. *Directory of Executive Recruiters,* published by Kennedy Publications, Templeton Rd., Fitzwilliam, NH 03447. Published yearly. Lists several thousand firms and the industries served.

2. *Directory of Personnel Consultants by Specialization (Industry Grouping).* Published by the National Association of Personnel Consultants, Round House Square, 3133 Mt. Vernon Ave., Alexandria, VA 22305, 703-684-0180.

The question is: do you **want** these lists, i.e., are they going to do you any good?

Well, let's say you decide to send recruiters your resume (unsolicited—they didn't ask you to send it, you just sent it uninvited). The average Executive Search firm will get as many as 1,000 such unsolicited resumes, or "broadcast letters," a week. Your chances of surviving? Well, *if* you currently make $75,000 or more per year, and *if* your resume and cover letter look *thoroughly* professional and well thought out, and *if* you send your resume to one of the larger executive search firms in this country, experts say you have a one in ten chance that they will contact you. On the other hand, the *first* to be eliminated will be those who a) are not presently on the level being looked for, or b) are not presently employed—even if they *are* on that level, or c) are not presently rising in their firm. That's why many experts say to the unemployed, in general: *Forget it!*

I do think it is necessary, however, to point out that things are changing in the Recruiting field. For one thing, onetime employment agencies now prefer to call themselves Recruiters or Executive Search firms. *(Employment agencies typically have to operate under more stringent state or federal regulations, hence the appeal of a different, less supervised, genre such as Executive Search.)* Whatever they call themselves, these new Recruiters/old employment agencies now represent employers; but are hungry for the names of job-hunters, and in many cases will interview a job-hunter who comes into the office unannounced or mails them a resume. I have known so-called Recruiters in some of the smaller firms who truly extended themselves on behalf of very inexperienced job-hunters. So, were I job-hunting this year, I think I would get one of the aforementioned Directories, look up the firms that specialize in my particular kind of job or field, and go take a crack at them. As long as you don't put all your eggs or hopes in this one basket, you really have nothing to lose—except some stationery and stamps.

Richard Nelson Bolles is the creator and author of the popular annual What Color Is Your Parachute, *from which this chapter was taken, with his permission (copyright © 1993 by Richard Nelson Bolles: published by Ten Speed Press, Box 7123, Berkeley, CA 94707). Over 4 million copies of this work have been sold, and it has been on* The New York Times *Best-Seller List for some six years!*

The Case for Mass Mailing to Executive Search Firms

by Don Baiocchi

Once you've definitely decided to leave your job (or have been terminated), and after you've reviewed your career plan and job-change strategy—by this time you've developed the "perfect" resume and cover letter—now comes the decision on how to make the first contact with executive recruiters as part of your multi-pronged overall plan.

How many and to whom should the cover letters and resumes be sent? Our view as outplacement counselors is that, if there are no geographical restrictions, the materials should be sent to every retained search firm's main and branch offices for starters—some 1,600 in total currently. We do this because we do not want to concede some 30% to 50% of the opportunities at any given time. We know from our experience that the full 1,600-piece mailing typically doubles the specific opportunity responses. In effect, targeting only the top 300 firms—as some outplacers recommend—normally results in about 50% of the responses of targeting 1,600. Costly, yes! But it is twice as effective!

Include Branch Offices

Why do we send the materials to each and every satellite office when we know that they end up at one central processing location? Because, when new searches begin in the "satellite" offices, the recruiters and researchers "pick off" the quick matches with incoming resumes. Once they get 25 or 50 or so, they cut off the retrieval process and begin contacting those 25 or 50. They will not go to the central processing location if they can satisfy their needs in their own satellite office. Another reason to mail to the satellite offices is that it takes up to a few months for a resume to work itself into the search firm's retrieval process; you could miss a few months of new searches.

Another feature of the 1,600 piece mailing is that it is not directed to a specifically named recruiter. It is addressed to the firm and its research department. The reason for this is because it is typically the fastest way to be "inputted" into the research system and therefore be accessible to all of the search firm's recruiters and researchers. It does not get delayed by a specific recruiter's travel, vacation, or just plain set aside in the "To Be Read" file.

Other Bases to Cover

We also recommend sending cover letters and resumes to specific recruiters, when appropriate, in addition to the 1,600 "generic" pieces. The obvious recruiters are those known personally to our candidate. In addition, though, we recommend sending letters and resumes to so-called "specialist" recruiters as appropriate. These "specialists" may be in functions (i.e., sales, law, etc.) or industries (i.e., chemicals, financial institutions, etc.). We maintain expansive "specialist" lists and it may be appropriate to substitute the specialist list for the generic list.

Other Possible Mailings

Finally, there are two other types of special mailings that may be appropriate. The first is the international search firm mailing. This may be appropriate if our candidate has an international background and either an interest in working in a specific geographical area of the world or in working for a company whose ownership is offshore. We have had considerable success with the international mailings over the past few years.

The second "other" type of special mailing is appropriate only for two types of executives: general managers with a strong P&L record and financial executives with strong control and SEC experience. Given this, it may be desirable to write to what we call "financial intermediaries." These are equity investors and venture capitalists, and we have a list of about 2,000 of them. We think they have between 20,000 and 30,000 companies in their portfolios, and we have been very successful in matching up general managers and financial executives with their portfolio companies through this kind of mailing. It needs to be sequenced after all of the other search mailings because more and more search firms are being hired by the financial intermediaries to help them with their executive needs.

Summary for Senior Executives

Up to now, we have described the executive search process and discussed the various types of mailings that executives in search of a position can make. These mailings can be quite extensive—and costly. They can number several thousand:

National generic search mailing	1,600
Specialist search mailing	50–1,000
International search mailing	600
Financial intermediaries	2,000
	5, 200

Some senior executives shy away from the thought of 5,000 resumes being mailed out to the world. We view it as a "press release" with a restricted circulation: 5,000 intermediaries representing 50,000 companies. How many will need the senior executive's services?

Approach for Lower and Middle Executives

The above extensive mailings apply to the more senior executives whose compensation levels are $100,000 to $125,000 on up. Executives whose compensation is in the $75,000 to $100,000 level may want to consider also doing a mailing to the contingency search firms. The specifics of these search firms are contained in the same directory as the retained search firm specifics, i.e., *The Directory of Executive Recruiters* published by Kennedy Publications: there are about 2,000 contingency firm main offices, plus over 800 branches, for a total of some 2,800 in all.

The entire contingency recruiter list should be considered if there are no geographic limitations. Obviously, if there are geographic and/or functional and/or industry limitations, *The Directory of Executive Recruiters* also identifies those. Hence the mailing can be more restricted if desired.

For those managers whose compensation levels are below $75,000, the contingency section of the *Directory* should be considered exclusively. The retained search firms normally kick in at $75,000 and above, but the contingency search firms will operate at the $25,000 to $75,000, with most focusing on the $40,000 to $75,000 levels.

Don Baiocchi of D.P. Baiocchi Assoc., Inc. in Chicago is a former executive search consultant now practicing corporate outplacement and management consulting. His text appeared originally in Baiocchi's Bulletin, *Vol. IX, No. 3, March 1995.*

How Recruiters Do—
and Do Not—
Fit into Your Job Search

by Mary Lindley Burton & Richard A. Wedemeyer

The Mystique of Executive Search

You are marketing you-the-product to one or more segments of the job market. In that market are brokers who match buyer and seller. These brokers have a variety of names: recruiter, headhunter, executive search consultant. In this chapter we refer to all people and firms providing this brokerage function as *recruiters*.

The recruiting industry has a certain mystique to many outsiders. Managers know that every day someone gets that unexpected call from a recruiter that can propel him or her into an exciting and rewarding new position. Many managers maintain contact with a handful of recruiters in hopes of one day receiving that magic call. Ironically, most managers are also aware of the questionable practices of some recruiters. Most people have at least one negative recruiter story—sometimes heard second- or thirdhand, sometimes a painful chapter in their own past.

Begin by learning the basics: how recruiters are compensated, who makes up the industry, their function as job-brokers, and how they do—and do not—fit into your job search.

> *My first move, after I was fired, was to contact several recruiters who had worked for our firm. They were friendly, but the weeks went by and nothing happened. Finally, I came to the realization that the recruiter works for* the *recruiter, not for you! That wasted a lot of time in my search.*

NUGGET: When you clearly understand the function and limitations of these brokers, you can use recruiters effectively in your marketing campaign. Failure to do so could result in missing out on some great jobs or in your being used by recruiters. Avoid the frustration caused by having unrealistic expectations of recruiters.

Recruiters Are Paid by the Employer

Recruiter or broker fees are paid by the *employer* (the *client*) for *presenting* properly qualified candidates to fill an employment need. Employers work through a third party for any of a number of reasons: confidentiality (both inside and outside the firm), better access to the employees of competitors, enhanced discipline to the process, greater objectivity in defining the position and assessing candidates, prescreening of prospective candidates, and less burden on staff. Since the fee is customarily *one-third* of the new hire's annual cash compensation, the client has determined that the cost of using a recruiter is justified by access to a better pool of candidates, faster and more objective results, and less wear-and-tear on management than if recruiting were handled in-house.

During your job search you may encounter firms who at first glance appear to be recruiters but offer a different kind of broker function: connecting you with the job market in exchange for a fee paid by *you*. These are *not* recruiters but comprise a shadow part of the industry dealing with (some might say preying upon) people looking for jobs. We recommend against using such services.

NUGGET: Recruiters work for the corporate and institutional *client* who pays the fee, not for you. Never deal with a recruiter who charges *you* a fee. Job seekers who speak of "my recruiter" or who expect recruiters to carry out their job campaigns for them don't understand how the game is played.

Two Categories of Recruiters

Recruiters can be grouped into two broad categories, according to the nature of the client relationship and compensation and expense reimbursement arrangements.

- *Retainer firms* have an exclusive on their assignments; no other firm is engaged to fill the position. Customarily they are paid one-third of their fee when the contract is signed to initiate the search, with the remaining two-thirds paid over the course of the assignment, whether or not the position is filled. Expenses incurred are reimbursed by the client company. Retainer firms may or may not specialize in certain fields or industries but generally will accept a search assignment in any field.
- *Contingency firms* may or may not have an exclusive assignment from a company. They are paid a fee *only* if they fill a position. Their expenses are often *not* reimbursed by the client. They may have good contacts in partic-

ular industries or segments of the job market and under extraordinary circumstances will "shop" a particularly attractive candidate.

The pros and cons of working with each type of recruiter depend on the goals of your campaign, your professional history and your seniority in your field. Retainer recruiters normally handle assignments for higher levels of management, and they generally have a more professional reputation. Contingency recruiters handle a wider range of situations and include in their ranks a broader cross-section of players, from the very successful and principled recruiter who has developed expertise and a niche to the individual in a tight financial situation willing to bend the rules for a fee.

Elegantly appointed offices may be enjoyable to visit, but you should focus on what role a recruiter can play in your marketing campaign. Contingency recruiters are capable of marketing someone who might earn them a fee even if they are not aware of any actual openings; this is seldom if ever done by a retainer firm, which works only on specific client assignments. The universe of recruiters is large and varied; the most recent *Directory of Executive Recruiters*[1] lists over 1,000 retainer firms and over 1,500 contingency firms in the United States. Within that group may be several who could assist your marketing campaign—and some who could complicate it. It's your job to know how to use the recruiter or broker effectively.

Whenever you are dealing with a recruiter, determine in which category he or she belongs. Ask early in the conversation, "Does your firm do contingency or retainer search?" Recruiters with *retainer* firms will indicate clearly that they do *only* retainer work; *contingency* recruiters will often respond, "We do *both*." Just knowing enough to ask that question is a signal to the recruiter that you would like to use—but not *be* used by—a job broker.

Responding to a Recruiter's Initial Contact

It's happened! You answer your phone to hear a professional-sounding voice say, "I'm Reg Percival with Truss Steward. We're working on a very interesting assignment for a client, and I'd appreciate your input and reaction. Is this a convenient time for you to talk?" You excuse yourself to close the door and return to the phone with anticipation. What to do next?

- It is best to talk with the recruiter now; he or she is making lots of calls, and you may not connect again. By this point you should have your priorities clear, your skill set firmly in mind, and the parameters most important to recruiters (such as your geographical flexibility) well considered. If you cannot speak at length say, "I'm in a meeting," take the recruiter's number, and establish a callback time.

1. Kennedy Publications, Templeton Road, Fitzwilliam, NH 03447

- *Listen* to what he or she has to say; don't be impatient to start your sales pitch.
- *Respond* to what has been said. Most likely the recruiter will describe the assignment and leave it to you to indicate interest yourself or mention the names of people you know who fit the specifications. In some cases the recruiter is not interested in you as a potential candidate but is "sourcing" —seeking only what names or information you might offer; this should be clear from his or her initial comments.
- *Indicate interest* if the position appeals to you. Ask some reasonable, intelligent questions that demonstrate your knowledge about the field generally or the function specifically. Do *not* probe for information that the recruiter says is confidential. Mention your most relevant qualifications; don't exaggerate. Respond to a reasonable number of relevant queries. Don't be preoccupied with selling yourself at this point. The recruiter is interested in you; *don't risk disqualifying yourself* by pushing yourself too aggressively.
- *Let the recruiter propose the next move.* Be prepared to set up an appointment or to hear, "We'll be back in touch with you." Quite possibly, the person with whom you are speaking is not the recruiter but works in the firm's research department. In that case, he or she will be reporting on you and other potential candidates to the recruiter, who will set up a face-to-face meeting. Your appointment may be with a senior recruiter who is the primary liaison with the client or with a more junior person doing preliminary screening.
- Be sure to *get the full name and contact information* of the person who called you: name, firm, mailing address, telephone, fax number. If within several weeks they have not followed up as indicated, you may wish to call them, although a lack of follow-through generally indicates a lack of interest.

Initiating a Contact with a Recruiter

As you are working on your marketing campaign, in all likelihood somewhere a recruiter is working on an assignment to fill your ideal job. How do you get in touch with that recruiter? Unfortunately, there is no sure way of gaining the attention of a recruiter working on a search assignment in your target area. However, do the following to increase the probability of coming to the attention of recruiters:

1. *Network, network, network!* The more people you have made aware of your availability and qualifications, the greater the chance that one of them

will mention your name to a recruiter working on an assignment along the lines of your interests.

2. In most job searches *sending your resume to recruiter firms* is an appropriate part of your marketing campaign; it involves a certain expenditure of time and money but may bring results. However, be realistic about the chance of results. Most recruiter firms are inundated by unsolicited resumes; the larger firms get *thousands* each week, overwhelming the process of categorizing and logging in resumes, let alone matching them with current searches. A resume sent to a smaller, less well-known recruiter firm is more likely to be read, although the number of searches per firm is smaller.

NUGGET: When sending your resume to a search firm, be practical, not fancy. Address a brief, businesslike letter to a specific individual. Summarize your interests, your compensation range, and your views about relocating.

---

3. Establish contact with *recruiters who have placed colleagues* in your target field or function. Understand that their *current* list of assignments may be in completely different fields; however, they may be aware of related assignments being worked on by other recruiters in their firm. Don't hesitate to call more than one good contact at a firm: communications within a firm, or even in the same office, are not always flawless.

4. *Research the contingency recruiters* who specialize in the sectors of the job market you have targeted. Contact them early in your selling phase; they can be a source of market intelligence, and they may choose to market you. Be sure you understand the ground rules and maintain control.

5. *Contact recruiters with whom you have a special relationship,* such as personal friends or recruiters who have worked for your current or former employer. They will no doubt be very supportive and may have some good advice. However, don't develop unrealistic expectations.

Pointers for Working Effectively with Recruiters

1. For recruiters, time is money. Don't waste their time.

2. You create a good impression with recruiters by being organized, by describing yourself in a clear, concise and objective fashion, and by dealing with them in a straightforward manner.

3. Many people disqualify themselves during the initial telephone screening because they are not prepared and rely on their ability to extemporize.

Prepare a script in anticipation of a recruiter calling, with a concise overview of your background, a skills summary, and a synopsis of your goals for this transition. You'll sound managerial and impressive in your comments.

4. If you are dealing with a contingency recruiter who is interested in marketing you, *proceed with caution and stay in control.* Some contingency recruiters have very good contacts and are respected in the industries they service. A well-placed telephone call to a prospective employer could net you a job. However, if your resume is mass-mailed around the industry by a recruiter with a bad reputation, it can cause considerable damage to your marketing campaign. Insist on ground rules in advance. For example, you might insist that any firm the contingency recruiter wishes to contact on your behalf be run by you first. If you have already made contact with the firm, you'll avoid any conflicts over fees and preserve your straight-line communications with a potential employer.

5. Most recruiters are hardworking and honest. However, as in any field, some recruiters behave irresponsibly and unethically. Learn the ropes and look out for yourself. Never let a recruiter submit a falsified resume on your behalf. Never let a recruiter pressure you into making a decision before you are ready. Think twice when a recruiter calls your spouse or significant other to plug a job he or she wants you to take. Most difficulties people have with recruiters are caused by poor communications, a lack of clear ground rules and erroneous expectations.

6. Some recruiters are not above taking advantage of prospective candidates who permit themselves to be exploited:

   - If you are working with a recruiter who repeatedly arranges interviews that you find ego-gratifying but seldom in line with your objectives, watch out! The recruiter may be using you to make a favorable impression on a client, even to string a client along until he or she finds a suitable candidate. You may elect to gain interviewing experience and exposure by taking such interviews, but examine your motives to be sure this is a good use of your times and energy.

   - Recruiters may contact you as a source of information on other people in your firm. Thinking that you are the object of the recruiter's interest and trying to make a favorable impression, you cooperate fully, only to be dropped after the recruiter has obtained the necessary sourcing information. *If the recruiter's focus is more on the company you work for than on you, gracefully exit the conversation!* For example, "I've got another call coming in. Please call me again if you have an assignment related to my interests. Good luck on this search."

   - Once the client likes a candidate, recruiters can be very persuasive in convincing him or her to take a position that is a force fit. Stay clear about your priorities and your goals for this transition. Don't compromise your objectives.

7. If you are looking for an entirely new line of work, recruiters are unlikely to help your marketing campaign. Recruiters are hired to locate and present candidates with qualifications and career paths directly related to the client's needs. Their role is not to make the case for the off-specs candidate.

8. If you are unwilling to relocate or are highly selective about geographic areas, recruiters will find you less attractive as a potential candidate. However, if you do have geographical criteria, *make them known to the recruiter early in the discussion.* All too often search firms have presented a candidate and the client made an offer, only to learn that the candidate of choice has decided against a move to a new location. There is no *surer* way of alienating recruiter and client.

9. Recruiters do not pursue candidates who are employed by companies on their current list of clients. This seldom affects the job searcher but is another reason to contact many recruiters rather than just a few.

Understand the "Courtesy Interview"

Shortly after you lose a job, a good friend may say, "I talked about you with Mary Stuart of Softwick and Strangles; they've done a number of searches for our firm. She said she'd be happy to meet with you." Wow! A personal introduction to a top-flight headhunter! You thank your friend.

On entering the impressive offices of Softwick and Strangles, you receive a warm welcome from the receptionist and are ushered into Mary Stuart's office. She is very friendly and interested in your situation, asks a lot of questions and makes some good suggestions. After a while her secretary reminds her it's time for another appointment, and you leave, expressing sincere thanks for her help and feeling very good about yourself.

Reflecting back on the meeting the next day, you realize that nothing specific was said about what the next step would be or what Mary Stuart would be doing for you. Still you're thinking, "Certainly it can't hurt to have someone like that on my side. As a matter of fact, this job search may not be as complicated a process as I had feared."

Quite likely, you won't be hearing from Mary Stuart soon, if at all. Your meeting is a service commonly offered by recruiters: the courtesy interview. A good client asks for help for a friend; to maintain the relationship the recruiter agrees to meet you. In some cases such meetings are a useful orientation to the job search process, with the recruiter giving practical advice and direction. The danger is that you may come away with completely unrealistic expectations, thinking the recruiter will take an active role in finding you a job.

High-level managers, with many friends in close contact with recruiters, may even go through a *series* of courtesy interviews and come away convinced that the phone will ring any day with a new job. Don't underestimate the negative impact of this thinking. In all likelihood none of the recruiters who were so pleasant and attentive had an assignment that matched your background and attributes. The more probable scenario is your waiting in vain, becoming frustrated and less and less sure of your marketability. Too often the real bottom line of courtesy interviews is the loss of valuable time and a devastating blow to your self-confidence when the balloon of unrealistic expectations bursts.

Directory of Executive Recruiters

The most current and complete listing of recruiters is published by Kennedy Publications, Templeton Road, Fitzwilliam, NH 03447. Call them at 603-585-6544 to order by telephone. They also supply pressure-sensitive mailing labels that can be purchased in subgroups of recruiter specialization and disks for PCs.

Executive Temporary Placement Firms

The temporary employee concept has expanded to include upper-level managerial and professional positions with the recent growth in the number of executive temporary or interim management firms. Interim executives are a logical option in turnarounds, in crisis management situations or under circumstances where the longer-term prospects of the position are unclear. Another advantage to the prospective employer is the speed with which the need is filled. When a prospective corporate client contacts such a firm with a specific need, the executive temp firm undertakes to provide a suitably qualified person within several weeks.

Interim placement jobs typically last for three to twelve months. Fees are comparable to recruiter fees, in the range of 30 percent of actual compensation, and paid by the hiring corporation—with additional fees if the interim placement results in a permanent hire, a fairly common occurrence.

Executive temp firms maintain lists of prescreened individuals, including job seekers, retirees, and others in transition. Of particular interest are people with clearly defined skills and a willingness to relocate on short notice. If you fit these criteria, you can find out more information on executive temp firms, including a current directory, from Kennedy Publications, (603-585-6544).

You now have a clearer understanding of these "facilitating agents" in the job market—the brokers who earn a living locating candidates for corporations. Use their services intelligently where appropriate; they can be valuable in your campaign. Keep your priorities uppermost and your self-esteem intact, and you'll avoid being used by them.

Mary Lindley Burton and Richard A. Wedemeyer have taught the Career Seminar for the Harvard Business School Club of Greater New York for over a decade. Mary heads Burton Strategies, providing career strategy to individuals, and Dick, after many years with Jim Henson Productions, is currently with Performance Advantage, Inc. in Norwalk, Conn.

What You Can Expect in the Search Process

by A. Robert Taylor

When you are contacted by an executive search firm as an executive rather than as a potential client, the consultant will usually have one of three purposes in mind. Either he wants to discuss your possible candidacy for one of his assignments or he is seeking your advice on potential candidates because he respects your knowledge, contacts and judgment or he wants to question you as a reference on a candidate whom he is considering. No matter which of these is his purpose, your first consideration should be your own reputation and image. Should this search firm and should this consultant be permitted to use your name and be entrusted with the information that you may give them? If you do not know the firm or the consultant, you would be wise to ask for and check their references before answering any of the consultant's questions.

When you are satisfied that you are dealing with a reputable firm, it is customary to cooperate with the consultant who contacts you. Most good executives who are approached as prospective candidates will at least listen to the description of the open position whether or not they are interested in a possible change. It makes sense to do so because the opportunity just might be the right one, whether or not you were thinking about making a change.

Very often, the consultant, initially, can provide only general information about his client and his assignment because of the need for strict confidentiality. He must not, usually, enable you to identify his client until he is given permission to do so by his client. This is one of the reasons why the search firm's reputation is so important to you. When the search firm is reputable, you can safely answer the consultant's questions. You are also free to refuse to go further when the client organization is finally identified to you, and you decide that you would prefer not to join it.

Normally, the consultant will describe his client and the open position in general terms and will immediately ask you whether you would be willing to explore the opportunity. At this point, and throughout your relationship with the search firm and its client, it is wise to be frank, truthful, discreet, and decisive. There are countless cases of immature executives who view the approach of an executive search consultant as an opportunity to apply leverage within their own organization. A typical example was a divisional director of quality control with a large defense contractor who, when contacted by a search consultant regarding a broader manufacturing position in another company, informed his boss, his peers, and his subordinates that he was being offered a much bigger job elsewhere. His boss viewed him as essential to the good performance of the division and reacted by raising his salary, broadening his responsibilities somewhat and making him eligible for stock options. Having gained so many points on that occasion, this executive, during the following 15 months, tried the same ploy again. It did not work a second time. His bluff was called. Furthermore, when his boss was promoted shortly thereafter, this executive was no longer considered as a possible replacement, largely because of his behavior in trying to pressure the company into giving him more. He also lost credibility with two major executive search firms who realized that he had been trying to use them to improve his situation with his present employer.

If the opportunity described by the consultant who contacts you sounds at all interesting, all that is necessary at this stage is to express a willingness to explore it further. There is no commitment implied yet by either side. The next step will probably be an initial interview by phone for the purpose of determining whether you fit the general profile of the position. This step especially makes sense when you and the consultant are in different cities or countries, thus making a face-to-face interview expensive and time-consuming.

In conjunction with the telephone interview, the consultant will ask for your resume. If you have one, it can save some of your and his time in providing essential information on your background. If you do not have one, there is no obligation to prepare a resume.

The face-to-face interview with the consultant will be arranged to suit your convenience. It could well be one of the critical incidents in your career. Although you are being sought after by the consultant, you would not have agreed to an interview unless you were interested. The impression that you make will determine whether you will be recommended to the consultant's client. Certainly, it does not make sense to convey a false image, but there are some basics that should be observed. Among these are being punctual for the interview, allowing plenty of time to find and reach the meeting place. Another basic that is often overlooked is dressing appropriately and being well groomed. For example, an executive in another area of the country was being considered for a key position at the New York headquarters of a blue-chip corporation. He arrived at the consultant's hotel room dressed in a bright blue suit with trousers that were too long, tan shoes, colorful socks, and a rather flamboyant shirt and tie. The interview was a short one, and he was politely rejected.

During interviews with the consultant and subsequently with his client's executives, the basic guidelines should be frankness, truthfulness, and discretion. It is important to be a good listener. Good judgment needs to be exercised on the information that you reveal about your current employer and position. It is normal, however, to openly answer all questions regarding your current compensation package. Otherwise, neither the consultant nor his client can determine whether they can afford you.

On the matter of compensation, a mistake that is often made is to attempt to give a global figure that encompasses all of the benefits and perquisites. A typical example was an executive who, when asked to describe his compensation package, replied that it amounted to approximately $200,000. Detailed questioning finally brought out that his base salary was $110,000, his most recent bonus was $23,000, and the rest was his inflated estimate of the value of the benefits, stock options, and company car. Such responses do not make a good impression. On the other hand, during the initial discussions with the consultant on the phone, his question about your compensation can, if you prefer, be answered by saying, for example, that you would not consider a move for less than $150,000 base salary plus a substantial bonus opportunity and attractive stock options and that the salary requested could be higher if the location were more expensive than your present area of residence. This enables the consultant to decide whether his discussion with you should continue. The details of your current compensation can then be given to the consultant when he interviews you in person.

When the consultant decides that you are a probable candidate for the position, he will usually discuss references with you. He will be interested in talking with people to whom you have reported and to others who have worked closely with you. Here again, the reputation of the search firm is so important. It is unlikely that a consultant with a top firm would misuse or mishandle the references that you agree upon. You would not, of course, permit him to talk to anyone in your present company until your resignation has been accepted. He would insist that you contact the other references, who are outside your organization, to obtain their agreement—and thus their assurance of confidentiality—before they are approached by the consultant.

From the first contact with the consultant, there is the basic question as to when you should inform your present employer that you are being considered for a position with another organization. The best answer is "not until you have formally decided to accept the new job or to reject it." If you tell them beforehand, you put yourself into a no-man's land in which you are somewhere between someone who is already on his way out and an executive to be intensively courted. If you are not, in the end, offered the position, you could be looked upon by your current organization as a disloyal reject.

Many executives who are effective in managing other people are quite inept in handling themselves when considering an offer involving a change of employment. Ordinarily, they thoroughly research a proposal and consider all possible eventualities from worst case to best case. Too often, when approached as a prospective candidate for another company, they do not ask enough questions about the organization that is offering the new opportunity or about the job that is being proffered. Even more frequently, they do not think through the situations that they may face when they inform their present employer of their decision to leave. As a result, they either allow themselves to be persuaded to change their minds and stay, thus unnecessarily putting a question mark within their present organization over their judgment and reliability, or they make a change with which they are subsequently disappointed.

Supposing that, during the course of the efforts to recruit you, your boss suddenly tells you that he has become aware that you are a candidate for a position with another company. The best response is to readily admit it, giving as little information as is possible within the bounds of diplomacy and to ask the question, "Wouldn't you agree to explore an attractive opportunity if you were approached by a good executive search firm?"

It is wise to have a firm commitment in writing from the prospective employer prior to resigning. It should be in the form of a contractual agreement that spells out all of the important aspects of the position, all details of the compensation package, and the organization's obligations in moving you, your family, and household. In addition, of course, an adequate period of notice of termination of employment should be specified.

When you are first approached by an executive search firm as a prospective candidate, you are probably one of very many executives on their list of prospects for the position. When you are presented to the firm's client organization, you may be one of only three candidates who are under serious consideration. If you are turned down along the way, try to determine the real reason so that you can learn from the experience. If you have established a good rapport with the consultant, he may well contact you again when he is asked to undertake a similar assignment.

A. Robert Taylor has been in executive search for over 25 years and pioneered the profession in Latin America with Boyden and TASA. He is currently senior vice president with A.T. Kearney Executive Search in Miami. This chapter is reprinted with permission from his book, How To Select And Use An Executive Search Firm, *copyright © 1984 by A. Robert Taylor and published by McGraw-Hill.*

Can Executive Search Firms Really Help?

by David Bowman & Ronald Kweskin

That depends on what level you have reached in your career. Unless you can qualify for a job that pays over $50,000 a year, most search firms will not be interested in you.

Understand that search firms find people for jobs, *not* jobs for people. That is a profound difference. Search firms do not work for you; they work for their client companies.

In fact, many search firms (as well as employment agencies) are becoming quite specialized in the industries or functions they serve. We see firms searching *only* for financial managers, or sales managers or managers in very specific industry fields such as entertainment, high tech or energy. As the information age grows and expands through the 1990s and into the year 2000, this trend toward specialization will continue. Today, it is almost impossible for any search firm manager to stay abreast of changes and new developments in more than a single field. This trend means that the job seeker soliciting search firms must be aware of their specializations in order to minimize wasted time, money and energy.

How Do Search Firms Get Paid?

A search firm is paid by an employer to find superior candidates for a particular job opening. The fee generally amounts to between twenty-five percent and thirty-five percent of the annual salary paid for the job. In other words, if the position pays $100,000 a year, the search firm stands to be paid a fee of between $25,000 and $35,000.

Actually, there are two types of search firms: retainer and contingency. The retainer firm enters into an exclusive arrangement with an employer to fill a particular opening. The firm is paid a percentage of the fee up front (before the search begins) and the remainder over the period of the search. A contingency firm is paid *only* if a candidate they have located is actually hired for the job. Theirs are non-exclusive arrangements, and it is common for a number of different contingency firms to be searching for candidates to fill the same job opening. Incidentally, contingency firms will occasionally handle positions that pay less than $50,000 a year, so if you are making less than this, it is a good idea to find out whether a firm is exclusively retained or contingency, because the former will not be interested in you but the latter may be.

How Do I Locate and Get in Touch with an Executive Search Firm?

First, try your local yellow pages. Search firms are usually listed under "executive search consultants" or sometimes under "management consultants" (but with these, phone before sending a resume—they may do other kinds of consulting, not executive searches). For a nationwide directory of executive search firms, refer to the *Directory of Executive Recruiters.* Your local library may have a copy, but if not you can order a copy from: Kennedy Publications, Templeton Road, Fitzwilliam, NH 03447 (603-585-6544).

Once you have identified a search firm, try to arrange an interview or meeting through a personal contact, someone who knows someone in the firm. If that fails, write a letter briefly outlining your experience and the type of position in which you are interested. Include a resume, and be sure to indicate the salary range that you need. Then follow up your letter with a telephone call a few days later. Be realistic about your chances, however. Many search firms receive hundreds of resumes each week. Only a very small percentage, perhaps as little as two to four percent, actually qualify for a position that the firm is attempting to fill at the time. And time is money to these people, so don't expect much attention.

Again, your chances for consideration will improve if you can somehow arrange a face-to-face meeting. You never know what assignments will come in next week or next month, and having seen you in person, the search executive is more likely to remember you.

Are Search Firms Really Worth the Bother?

Sure. Just don't pin all your hopes on finding a job through one of them. If you meet the standards necessary to qualify for consideration by search firms, you have nothing to lose by contacting as many as possible. Our advice is to send a letter and resume, then call and try to arrange a meeting. If you can't arrange a meeting, forget that firm; they will call you if you fit a search they are conducting.

However, here is some good advice. Before you send your resume to a search firm, phone to see who is in charge of your specialty, your functional area. Tell that person's secretary that you will be sending a resume. That way, you will be writing to a partner or senior manager, rather than letting a lower-level researcher decide whether you are kept or "trashed."

If a Search Firm Calls Me, How Should I Respond? What Do I Tell Them?

Assuming you have gotten a message and are to call them back, be sure to place the call from a quiet, private place. If they are calling you, and if you have no office door to shut, call them back at a better time—that is never a problem. Next, be honest. Don't be coy or secretive, or try to "expand" your degrees, experience, responsibility or titles. These folks have ways of trapping you, and if you haven't been straight, they will drop you like a hot potato. You'd better be honest about your salary, too. Also, don't expect free advice or an overly long conversation. Answer the recruiter's questions quickly, but with an eye to the problems you have solved and the *real* responsibilities you have had.

Ask if the recruiter has an assignment, and probe as to what it is and how you might fit. Even if the job is way off base, try to meet with the headhunter. After all, even though the current search may not fit you, tomorrow is another day, and maybe there will be a search that *will* fit. And, a personal meeting always puts you a step ahead, because now the headhunter has you in the computer. Also remember that legitimate executive recruiters are *always* paid by the *employer*. If a recruiter asks you for money, such as a registration fee, hang up!

Then, too, there are a lot of "one-man-bands" in the search business. Some of these folks work out of their homes and/or phone booths. This doesn't mean they are not competent; it simply means they are small. Therefore, don't expect them to have a long list of clients, and don't spend a long time or pin a lot of hopes on one of them. Going in to see their offices can usually give you an idea about the size of a recruiting firm.

Once I Have Been Called by a Search Firm, How Soon Will I Know If I Am a Candidate for a Job?

That depends on a lot of factors. For example, you may be eliminated for various reasons after your initial conversation, or you may end up a finalist among a selected few being considered for the position. The time frame is somewhat controlled by how long the search has been active at the time you are called. If contact is made at the beginning of the search (a search may take between two and six months to complete), the recruiter and employer may not be anxious to narrow the field until more candidates have been uncovered. On the other hand, if you are called midway into the search, or after they have been working on it for a considerable length of time, you can expect some pretty quick action. When you are called, simply ask the recruiter how long he or she has been working on the search.

Sometimes a problem can occur when the final three to five candidates are presented to the client company, but the client can't make up its mind. In this case, two things can happen: either more time is needed for interviewing the finalists, or none are chosen (which may mean the search goes back to square one). In a nutshell, you never know how long the process will take.

If I Send My Resume to One Office of a National Search Firm or Employment Agency, Will It Be on Their Computer for Other Offices?

Maybe, but don't count on it. Search firms get such huge volumes of resumes each week that they only computerize a small percentage of them. So play it safe, and send your resume to the search firm office in each city you are considering, just to be sure.

David Bowman is the founder and president of TTG Consultants in Los Angeles, a human resources consulting firm specializing in the management of corporate and career change. Ronald Kweskin is a senior vice president of the firm.

This chapter is reprinted with permission from their book: *Q: How Do I Find the Right Job? A: Ask the Experts,* copyright © 1990 by John Wiley & Sons, Inc.

A Word to Executives Open to Change . . .

Remember that executive recruiters are paid by management and must be so oriented. They rarely interview unless with a specific job in mind, and most do not even acknowledge resumes. If you're lucky enough to have qualifications matching a recruiter's current assignment, however, the road to an interview can be almost instantaneous.

A few cautions:

- **Don't telephone to follow up:** This is a waste of your time and an annoyance to the recruiter.
- **Don't walk in and expect an interview.**
- **Don't attempt to fool anyone on present or expected salary level.** These experts have a way of zeroing in on the truth. Frankness and honesty is the best policy.

While some recruiters file over-the-transom resumes, most don't. **So repeat in six months if you are still in the market.** And don't take any listed salary minimums too literally— merely use as a general guide.

One last word: the recruiter as a professional must respect the confidence of your situation. This is automatic. If you have any doubts, don't venture out. There is always a remote possibility of a slip-up, but this is a chance you have to take once you have decided to test the market or make a change.

GOOD LUCK!

Five Easy Pieces of Advice on Dealing with Executive Recruiters

by James H. Kennedy

1. Start relating to recruiters in your field long before you need them or they call you.
2. Check them out if you've never heard of them.
3. In your first week of orientation on a new job, tell your new boss not to get upset if he hears you've talked with a recruiter or a resume shows up: "They're calling me all the time."
4. Never lie or even stretch the truth about education, job experience, salary, etc.
5. Level with the recruiter if you'd entertain a counter-offer to stay.

James H. Kennedy is founder, editor and publisher of Executive Recruiter News.

Profile of a Headhunter

by William R. Wilkinson

Your typical headhunter looks mostly like you and me, provided you are a male WASP between thirty-five and sixty and you identify with the executive public at large. Some recruiters are tall, well-dressed, debonair, polished, "tennis, anyone?" types; others are short and round with food spots on their ties and pants badly in need of pressing. A few appear to be fast-talking city slickers, and maybe are. Others are slower moving clod-kicker types who punctuate their questions and comments with hesitation and who like to laugh a lot. Most are happily married family men who mow their own lawns on Saturdays and shoot an occasional 113 at their country clubs. About a third have been divorced and remarried. Almost all aspire to have their children graduate from good colleges and marry talented mates.

The more successful ones have a great deal in common: They are intellectually bright, socially adept, sensitive and quick in forming good judgments about man-job matches or mismatches, and they know either in person or over the telephone just about everybody they need to know to conduct their businesses well.

Generally, all of them can be found, when at work, garbed in at least one article of Brooks Brothers clothing. Their backgrounds are varied. Many had their early training and experience in the personnel relations field; still others cut their teeth in consumer goods marketing, general management in almost any field, or management consulting. Almost all of the highly successful recruiters' backgrounds contain an exposure to sales of a product or service. Some are Ph.D. psychologists. At least one is a former medical doctor. A few are attorneys who either disliked or failed at law. Virtually all once were executives themselves. Not even a handful are trained engineers or accountants, whose tendencies to think more in the realm of black and white than of unpredictable human behavior tend to disqualify them from evaluating people expertly. Contrary to publicity, almost none are college students, the temporarily unemployed, or housewives—the business is easy to crack, but not that easy.

Headhunters share other characteristics as well. They like to work on short-term assignments whose results can be quickly and observably measured and enjoyed. They have a penchant for living in suspense and by their wits, and they cannot abide for long what they portray as the predictable stability that characterizes ordinary executive jobs. They thrive on the stimulation and prestige of rubbing shoulders with industry, business, and private sector decision makers and leaders; most can hold their liquor as well as or better than the candidates they interview. The successful ones are self-motivated and compulsively hard working, accustomed to breakfast and dinner interviews, weekend phone calling, and living out of a suitcase. They take vacations, but never far from a telephone, and rare is the experienced headhunter who has not memorized Ma Bell's area code book and most of his clients' phone numbers.

They have even more in common: Their educational backgrounds run the gamut of average to superior, with probably over half being MBAs, and many have attended the "right" schools. (One search firm headquartered in the east boasts a strong majority of Yale graduates.) Not only are headhunters degreed; their knowledge of the intimacies of dozens of occupations in scores of businesses is superior, thanks to the handling of an extreme variety of search assignments in countless industries. Many are equipped to discuss in detail (although with no expertise) over breakfast with a candidate the manufacture of hybrid integrated circuits, at lunch with another the current practices in fast food merchandising, and over cocktails with still another the laws and trends pertaining to mortgage banking. They must know the businesses of their client companies to represent them with competence, and they try hard to do so. At the very least, they have learned to excel in the use of the buzz words common to their clients' industries.

They are versatile in other ways as well. On the whole, they have excellent memories for names and faces; they know how to budget their time and travel, where to stay, and the better restaurants almost everywhere; and they are tactful masters of the art of using their airline smarts to get a seat on any oversold flight on which they failed to make a reservation. They write mellifluous business letters and reports with ease, they are selective in hiring secretaries who know how to charm everybody, and they have the believable sincerity of conviction to assure each client that his is their most interesting and challenging assignment and each candidate that he is very much in the running.

The headhunters' skill in amateur industrial psychology is unsurpassed by other amateurs in the field. Their interview style, using questions beginning with the words "who," "what," "when," "where," "why," and "how," is contrived to avoid the stereotypic "yes" or "no" answer; and probing is their learned substitution for accepting a response at face value.

The art of matching person and job demands far more of them than just finding a candidate or two with the right experience. The candidate must "fit" in other ways as well. A client company's president, formerly an all-American football player from Ohio State, may want a Casper Milquetoast as his vice president of finance, not another all-American jock with whom he must share a fading spotlight; or the compulsive, fingernail-biting vice president of manufacturing might explain that he wants an outgoing, hail-fellow-well-met for his production manager, not one of those "introspective types" who chew his nails. Of course, the headhunter must recognize without voicing his opinion that the only man acceptable will be a carbon copy of his client. Skill is required to recognize a good Casper Milquetoast or obsessive fingernail-biter when you see one.

Recruiters also are adept at handholding (called "client handling" in the trade) anxious client company officers who are convinced that things are not moving fast enough or are moving too fast. They have learned the knack of explaining the inexplicable, placating the implacable, soothing the rough sea, or stirring up the mill pond to set client or candidate minds at rest. Although they cannot duplicate Merlin's skill, they excel at trying.

On behalf of their clients, the headhunters have become skilled and innovative negotiators in matters pertaining to salaries, fringe benefits, bonuses, stock options, and other imaginative forms of compensation to concoct pay packages that will attract the selected candidate. A few have been justifiably accused by their clients of "giving away the shop" to make compensation more appealing; most do not. Their orientation is management's, not the candidate's; besides, they want repeat engagements for doing a job well.

Finally, headhunters pride themselves on being just plain good businessmen, and most are. My observation is that, on the whole, they are interesting people and real, and they count among their friends the business people with whom they have become close, clients and candidates alike.

William R. Wilkinson has over 35 years of experience as an executive recruiter and in the 60s headed a premier firm, Wilkinson Sedwick & Yelverton, Inc. He is now in the smaller, more personalized mode that he prefers, as Wilkinson & Ives in San Francisco. His book, Executive Musical Chairs, *copyright © 1983 by William R. Wilkinson, Warrington & Co., from which this chapter was taken, earned these comments in* Executive Recruiter News: *"Spiced with wit, leavened with common sense: a smorgasbord of practical ideas and insights for candidates, recruiters and clients."*

How to Enlist the Support of an Executive Recruiter

Sending an unsolicited resume makes sense if you qualify

by Tony Lee

Executive search firms carry a mystique that often deters jobhunting managers from making unsolicited contact. Candidates tend to believe that recruiters are too inaccessible or specialized to have interest in a resume that arrives over the transom. Such a belief couldn't be more wrong, say recruiters.

Almost every reputable search firm saves the resumes it receives from job hunters. The advent of computerized record keeping allows firms to categorize arriving resumes by industry, specialty, location and compensation level, and retain them indefinitely. In the event that a person's qualifications closely match the needs of a client company, chances are good the candidate will be contacted, recruiters say.

"If you have the right qualifications at the right time, it makes sense to contact search firms because it's possible you could be brought into the loop of a search," says Paul R. Ray Jr., president of recruiters Paul R. Ray & Co., based in Fort Worth, Texas. "My philosophy is, nothing ventured, nothing gained."

Alfonso Duarte agrees, saying the economics of contacting recruiters are particularly sound. "Every avenue should be explored and since it only costs so little for a stamp, it's worth sending a resume to us," says the vice president of Korn/Ferry International in New York, the nation's largest search firm.

Do You Earn Enough?

To be sure, not every resume mailed to a recruiter is entered into the firm's database. The criteria for inclusion are strict throughout the industry, with a large percentage of unsolicited resumes weeded out each day. Salary level is the biggest hurdle.

"We cull unsolicited resumes for our database by salary first, with $75,000 as the minimum accepted level," says Mr. Duarte, who estimates that his firm receives 1,000 resumes a week, 300 of those at its New York office. While the salary level is lower at some Korn/Ferry offices in other parts of the country, Mr. Duarte says managers earning below $75,000 annually should concentrate on reaching contingency rather than retained search firms. (Retained search firms are hired by client companies to fill a specific opening and are paid regardless of their success. Contingency search firms are paid only if the candidate they represent is hired.)

The next hurdle faced by job hunters is how their resumes and cover letters are viewed by each firm's research department, which is where most unsolicited resumes are forwarded. Correspondence that's poorly written, full of typographical errors or unconventional in format or style is eliminated immediately from consideration, says David Richardson, executive vice president of Chicago-based recruiters DHR International.

"Assuming that a person is at the right salary level, we contact about 10%" of the job hunters who submit resumes, "unless they've given a half-hearted effort in their letter and resume," says Mr. Richardson, whose firm recently incorporated the Chicago offices of Boyden International. A poorly conceived resume or cover letter demonstrates a lack of effort and ability and is justification enough for throwing it away, he says.

A resistance to relocating is another barrier that excludes some candidates from consideration. Few recruiters limit their clients to one geographic area. By sending your resume to a recruiter, therefore, you implicitly acknowledge your willingness to move for the right opportunity, says Mr. Ray in Fort Worth. His advice to job hunters: "Think seriously about whether you'd relocate and under what circumstances before becoming involved in a search."

When trying to set an effective strategy for contacting search firms, applicants should follow a few guidelines, recruiters say. First, call recruiters who may have contacted you in the past. Even if you rebuffed their advances before, you aren't necessarily eliminated from future consideration. Next, talk to co-workers and other managers in your industry. "Ask if they've ever been contacted and get the names of specific recruiters for you to write to," says Mr. Ray.

If your network doesn't turn up a recruiter's name, you're left to choose between two approaches: rifle and shotgun. "Candidates who feel they're in the senior-level national or international job market should take a broad approach and contact all of the largest search firms. Those are the types of positions they specialize in," says James H. Kennedy, a Fitzwilliam, N.H.-based consultant and publisher.

"It's awfully hard for an individual to find out which recruiter specializes in the cat food industry at Heidrick & Struggles in Chicago, for example. Therefore, they should use a shotgun rather than a rifle approach when sending resumes and try to hit as many search firms as possible," says Mr. Kennedy, whose publications include Executive Recruiter News, a monthly newsletter and the annual Directory of Executive Recruiters.

Middle managers, on the other hand, and senior staff specialists typically have better luck contacting smaller, more specialized search firms. "The top 100 firms by and large are generalists. They're relationship-oriented not industry-oriented," says Mr. Richardson in Chicago. "Of those, the top 40 receive material from every possible source: outplacement firms, universities, senior executives." By focusing on smaller firms, he says, you increase the odds of being called and receiving personalized attention if you match a client's needs.

A Matter of Contention

Whatever size of search firm you decide to target, how you get your resume into the right hands is a matter of contention. Some firms actively discourage follow-up telephone calls while others advocate a personal follow-up. "To zero in on the right person to contact, it's a hell of a good idea to call each firm and ask who specializes in your industry," says Mr. Richardson. "You might get the name of a research director, from whom you can find out if there's one person or one office that handles more searches in your field," he says.

Paul Ray Jr. hopes few job hunters adopt this strategy. "It's a hassle to have people follow up by phone. We receive from 500 to 1,000 resumes a week, and we'd be on the phone all the time" if even a small percentage tried to call, he says.

If your efforts to enlist a recruiter's support are successful, Mr. Ray offers a checklist of points to be considered that can make your relationship with the search firm more effective. Those include:

- Remember that the primary objective of a retained search firm is to serve the client, not the candidate.
- Be candid up-front concerning your background, education and salary level. Those facts will be verified later on.
- If a position isn't of interest to you, say so immediately and ask to be kept in mind when a better match arises. You will be called when that occurs, he says.
- Ask about the firm's past business experience working in your industry or function before agreeing to interview.
- Ask for specific job information about responsibilities, exposure to top management, company culture and the compensation package, but realize that not all information can be divulged during the early stages of a search.

- ■ If you aren't invited to interview, understand that it isn't a reflection on you personally. It's probably just not the right situation for you in this case, Mr. Ray says.

Tony Lee is editor of the National Business Employment Weekly.

Five Ways to Alienate Recruiters

by Gabrielle Solomon

Meetings with executive recruiters are as important as any job interview—if not more so, since a recruiter may influence your career longer. So be on your best behavior, pre pare an inventory of your best skills, focus on your real strengths, make sure you're understood, never lie (it could be cause for termination later) and be realistic. Remember, recruiters are like matchmakers. Show your true self and you're more likely to end up in a great relationship.

To prevent disaster, review the following five sure-fire ways to blow your chances when meeting with headhunters, courtesy of Mark Fierle, vice president of executive search with the Jennings Co., an outplacement firm based in Irvine, CA:

1. Be blase about the meeting. Come dressed in casual clothes (shorts and sneakers, perhaps), slouch in your chair, make outrageous statements and explain, "Of course, I'd never say that in a 'real' interview."

2. During the conversation, act defensive and unprepared. To make sure the "real" you isn't revealed, evade questions whenever possible. Better yet, respond to tough queries by telling the recruiter to refer to your resume. Hey it took hours to compile, so why not let it speak for you?

3. Fudge on your resume. Since everybody does this, you'll just be missing out if you don't claim an advanced degree (even if you never finished your thesis), take full responsibility for team accomplishments, embellish job titles and extend your employment dates.

4. Sound like a jack-of-all-trades. You need a job and the recruiter needs to fill a slot, so who cares what you've actually done before? Once you're in front of the employer, you'll find a way to make yourself sound qualified.

5. Demand a superstar salary, job title and responsibilities. You want the best, and this isn't the time to be practical. Aim for the moon.

Gabrielle Solomon is associate editor of the National Business Employment Weekly.

13 Tips on Responding to Executive Recruiters

by James H. Kennedy

1. Have a clear career game plan and job-changing mindset before you get the call. (This includes always having an up-to-date resume.)
2. Be open but cautious.
3. Ask questions to help you determine the recruiter's legitimacy, credibility, reputation and modus operandi (i.e. contingency or retainer, exclusive assignment or not, professional affiliations, office location).
4. Never stretch the truth: about job experience, education, income, etc.
5. Bow out early if you're really not interested: offer to be a resource if not a candidate.
6. Do your homework on the client organization, once identified. (The recruiter should provide basic material such as the Annual Report, but go beyond to clippings, trade publication stories, etc.)
7. Don't play hard to get. Keep appointments, return calls, cooperate.
8. Sign the reference-checking authorization if presented: it proves you have nothing to hide.
9. Cover yourself at work: despite all precautions and confidentiality, slip-ups sometimes occur. Tell your superiors you're always getting calls from recruiters, but that it doesn't mean you're looking.
10. Don't cultivate an offer just to get leverage where you are: such short-term, self-serving strategy usually backfires.
11. Of 200 "suspects" uncovered in initial research, perhaps 50 will make the first cut, five will be finalists, 1 will get the job. Don't take it personally: the search process aims for a perfect fit, and it's probably in your best interests anyway.
12. Don't burn your bridges: with the recruiter or with your present employer.

13. Let the recruiter run interference for you: on salary and benefits and perks. While compensated by the hiring organization, the search consultant can be your advocate, too, and has a stake in your success.

James H. Kennedy is founder, editor and publisher of Executive Recruiter News.

What to Do When Headhunters Call . . . and How to Cultivate Long-Term Relationships with Them

by John Sibbald

Whether you use resumes with smart cover letters or the intercessions of contacts, sooner or later your efforts with executive recruiters will be rewarded with a call or letter from some of those on your target list. When this happens, you can consider yourself to be on the brink of being in the recruiter's system. You want that more than anything. Most often the first communication from the headhunters you're trying to cultivate will come in the form of a telephone call. How you handle the contact determines your chances of becoming a prospect, and perhaps later a candidate, to that recruiter.

The best recruiters do not make idle telephone calls. When one calls you, you can be sure that the recruiter is doing one or more of these three things: (1) sounding you out as a possible candidate, (2) determining whether you might be a source—in other words, whether you can suggest a candidate or two for one of the searches the recruiter is handling, or (3) repaying a favor to a client, former client, prospective client, a prior placement, a fellow recruiter, a current candidate or a gadfly. Regardless of the recruiter's motives for calling you, do something on your end of the line to cause that recruiter to have good reason to either arrange a personal visit or make a mental note to keep in touch with you. In brief, don't squander the opportunity to make yourself memorable to that headhunter.

Let's take the optimal situation. One of North America's top recruiters is calling you. She's phoned you after reading your resume, which had been referred to her by the firm's research department. You had written her after discovering that she specialized in your line of work. Your recruiter passes along some other background on the opportunity, and it all sounds interesting to you. You know you want a personal interview, but you also know that you do not want to sound overly eager.

Be savvy but not coy. You don't have to go through the normal ritual of determining whether the headhunter calling you is reputable if she's profiled in my book, *The New Career Makers*. In fact, she's one of the top 2 percent in the business. After her first description of the job to you, she will have some reasonably probing questions to ask you over the telephone. She needs to be as sure as she can be that she doesn't waste her time or her client's dollars on a very costly face-to-face interview.

Be prepared to respond to questions that attempt to fix the current scope of your responsibilities and the structure and nature of your current or past employer. If you've listened well when the recruiter first described her need to you, you'll pick up on some of the key background and personal experience factors the recruiter must find in your background in order to qualify you as a viable candidate. Headhunters are working from what they call a specification, or candidate profile—an outline that highlights the must-have and desirable-to-have features in a prospect's background.

Further along in the conversation your recruiter is going to inquire about your willingness to relocate, whether children and a working spouse are involved, and at least some idea of what your compensation requirements are going to be. Make no mistake about it—your recruiter is still just sizing you up against the job specifications. She'll also ask you such delicate-to-deal-with questions as why you're looking for a new position and, if you're currently out of work, the names of your most recent superior and others who know your work and circumstances. Obviously, it's wise that the reason you give for being between jobs—or "on the beach," as the recruiters put it—jibes with what your boss says. And you can be quite sure that your recruiter is going to run a reference check on you with your last superior before having you visit for a personal interview.

I hope you win your interview, and I wish you good luck with it. There is one tip I might offer: if your interview happens to be with one of the top recruiters profiled in my book, it would be smart for you to review the recruiter's profile before you make your visit. That way you might avoid the rather awkward moment that I experienced a few years ago with a job seeker who wanted to leave me with a nice personal touch. The interview happened to be in the fall, during football season, and he smiled broadly at me as he was exiting my office. Then he suddenly thrust out a big hand and chanted, "GO BIG RED!" I was momentarily stunned. Then it dawned on me. I had graduated many years ago from the University of Nevada. He had apparently misread my school somewhere as the University of Nebraska. Oh well; it was a nice try. Both schools do start with "Ne."

Cultivating a Long-Term Relationship with Recruiters

As anyone who has ever been the recipient of a pink slip could tell you, the best time to start looking for a job is before you have to. So perhaps you're one of the very fortunate who still has a job, but you're not happy or fulfilled in it. Or maybe you're still hanging on as a middle manager in some organization that has not quite flattened its organizational structure enough yet to compress you into escape velocity. But you can see it coming and you want to prepare for the worst.

It's never too soon to start building that all-important relationship with North America's top headhunters. Once again, you must start with the identification of the right executive recruiters—those whose recruiting interests coincide with your own employment interests. It's a matter of creating your personal target list of recruiters to cultivate, as outlined earlier in this chapter. Then comes the ongoing process of becoming known to the right recruiters and helping them create a file on you that causes them to call you on every search they do that is in your field of interest and aspirations.

The first step, of course, is getting your well-crafted resume into the hands of the right recruiters. Your cover letter with a compelling handle helps you accomplish this critical step. Maybe the first call-back from a headhunter will be right on target. But chances are better that it will be about a job in which you neither would fit nor be interested. Let's say your call is from a recruiter who is looking for the new general manager of the Detroit Athletic Club. You happen to be managing one of America's top country clubs. You know how difficult it is today to run a successful city club. You also have the wisdom to realize that with the dues deductibility issue and the major shift in member lifestyles, city clubs of all types are having significant difficulties. An then, of course, there is the issue of working in downtown Detroit. Besides, you like to get in an occasional round of golf, which you can do on Mondays at your current club. Do you just say, "No, Mr. Recruiter, I'm not interested," and hang up? No; instead, you put your mind in gear to help that headhunter with a suggestion.

A light bulb goes on in the recesses of your memory, revealing seldom-used but hopefully useful facts, and out comes a response like this: "I'm sorry I'm not quite right for your search, but I do have a suggestion of a possible candidate for you. Mortimer Clubhead and I went to school together at Michigan State, one of the top hotel and restaurant schools in the country. He is also a CIA graduate. Incidentally, that's the Culinary Institute of America, not the less reputable outfit you might be thinking of. He's been at the Cosmopolitan Club in New York for the last twelve years. He runs one of the best city clubs in the country. He grew up in Michigan, and I know he would like very much to get back there. Would you like to know more about him?" Of course your recruiter friend would.

Or maybe your response is along these lines: "Try as I might, I don't have a single individual to suggest to you as a candidate, but I can give you the names of a couple of terrific sources. They manage top athletic clubs themselves, so they aren't recruitable, but they know everybody who ever ran a gourmet dining club or bounced a hard rubber ball off the wall of a squash court." In addition, you might know of the various club management journals and the association to which virtually all club managers belong. Whatever you do, leave that recruiter whom you have worked so hard to cultivate with food for thought—and a nice warm feeling that you are a very worthwhile contact. Your name and phone number will go into the recruiter's workbook as a good source, someone for him to call again.

Then, as fate would have it, a week later you bump into Sally Donovan, the manager of your own city's athletic club. She had heard about the search at the Detroit Athletic Club and told you that she might have some personal interest but didn't know who to contact. You promptly follow up with your recruiter friend by phone with Sally's home telephone number and some complimentary comments of your own about her. By this time most of the top recruiters will very likely have started a file on you even if you have not yet become a candidate on any of their searches.

Now it's a matter of gently but regularly stuffing the file folder with your name on it in that headhunter's office. You're in no immediate hurry to make a change, but you do want to know when an exceptional opportunity opens up. Your recruiter will not only add items to your file but will also store key elements from your background in a computer. This data will be available for years to come not only to that recruiter but to all other search consultants in his firm and those in branch offices.

Don't be concerned if no acknowledgments come from your recruiter. Keep adding to his file on you. Some always-helpful items are news releases or publications that talk about your activities or clippings from a trade journal that has an article referring to you or a new program you've launched. If you happen to be with a government agency, school system, college or university, hospital, hotel or association, the same logic holds. Take advantage of articles and stories that talk about you and what you are responsible for. Please do not send complete curricula that you've worked on for your high school, a copy of the Federal Budget for the United States of America with a paper clip on the page that refers to your department in a footnote or the membership directory for the University Club—copies of each of which I received in the past.

Annual reports can be good or bad. Unless you are president, chairman or the vice-president of communications responsible for its production, do not send the full report. Select a summary page from the financials or those pages from the president's letter or from the report somewhere that refer to you and your department. Annual reports pollute headhunter's offices and take up valuable space in the circular files and recycling bins already overflowing with the monsoons of ill-directed resumes raining down upon America's recruiters.

Periodically, it's wise to update your resume and be sure you get it in the hands of every executive recruiter you've been able to build a relationship with. Try attaching a short note to it that says something along these lines: "Just thought you'd like to add this most recent resume of mine to your file. My current compensation is a base of $75,000 with a bonus paid last February of $15,000. I remain keenly interested in a general manager position in a top country club in the desert."

Now what's this we hear? You've won election to your local school board. Or you've been selected for the board of the Club Managers Association of America. That is major news for your file, so send it in. Membership, but especially leadership, in your association is one of the most important credentials you can add to your attributes in furthering your relationship with those on your target list. One of the most well-worn directories in any recruiter's office is the *Encyclopedia of Associations*. Few searches neglect contacting the leadership of trade associations or professional societies. The fact that your peers think enough of you to elect you to a leadership role in your field of work is one of the very strongest credentials any professional can have. Broadcast it.

In the final analysis, what every smart professional is really after is *visibility* with those recruiters on your target list. Very few of us become renowned in our own field. We can dream about writing an article or a book or making a scientific discovery of great merit that catches everyone's attention. But most of what goes into our file with our headhunter friends will be a steady accumulation of little things that eventually add up to a significant record of achievement. Never forget that visibility can also be acquired by what Daniel Patrick Moynihan has called "creeping gradualism." It may not be as exciting as achieving instant fame, but it often proves far more enduring.

As one might expect, some things will go into your file that you have not provided or even knew that your recruiter contact had. The headhunter you're out to win over will have made a note and put it in your file if you were abusive, devious, or pushy with his secretary. Or maybe he noticed that you wore short socks to your interview with him or that you bathed in so much cologne that he got a headache from it and couldn't work the rest of the day. Like many firms, my own has a form in which we evaluate every person we meet on such subjective factors as presence, energy level, listening ability, language facility, and many other personal factors. This too goes into your file, although you will never see it. So will copies of the reference reports the recruiter does on you, including verification of your college degree—the single biggest item of candidate fabrication today, and yet one of the easiest things for employers to check.

Perhaps you "forgot" in your resume to add a former employer you had for less than a year; a recruiter from your target list may discover this and add the information to your file. Or you might have made a "simple error" in calculation and overstated your earnings by 30 to 40 percent. When the recruiter uncovers that tidbit, another entry goes into your file. A cardinal rule for every headhunter is *no surprises for a client.* Your headhunter's entire reputation as a top professional rests on thoroughness. The best sniff out every fabrication.

It is hard for me to confess this, but even these top search consultants have an endemic weakness. They are not very forgiving when a job seeker takes advantage of them. It is difficult for headhunters to build a relationship with a client and then win a search from that client. Recruiters do not take it kindly when a job seeker lets them down in a way that jeopardizes the relationship between consultant and client—or, worst of all, ends it.

Two of the most common embarrassments that recruiters suffer through are (1) when a candidate's spouse or family will not move after the breadwinner has proceeded all the way to the altar and received an offer, and (2) when a candidate has received an offer from a new employer and then used that to extract a counteroffer from the old employer. Although black balls tend to take up too much file space, Avery Label makes a nice flat black dot that applies very neatly to an individual's file folder. Only the most foolish would risk that censure with any of the top recruiters. Many a professional who has taken advantage of a recruiter has discovered that even elephants don't survive as long as the memory of a headhunter wronged.

Fortunately, nothing like this is going to happen to you. You are out to develop the most positive possible relationship with the headhunters in your future. You know that every placement of these top recruiters at one time was nothing more than a name on the recruiter's long list of initial possibilities on that search. Somehow they prevailed over all the others. Each had a file started on them in that recruiter's office, probably years before they were placed. They very likely had files in other recruiters' offices too. Some had been placed by headhunter after headhunter throughout their rise to the top.

Many of America's top executives in every field of work have never really had to look for a job, even though they've had a number of different employers. The opportunities always came to them. In an increasing number of instances, the bearers of glad tidings were the headhunters they had met and cultivated along the way. Wouldn't it be nice to have the feeling that even while you have your head down working away at your current grindstone, someone out there is constantly sensitive to you and your aspirations? Your recruiter friends would be minding your career for you.

Even after you've succeeded in taking a new position with the help of a recruiter, don't just close the door on a relationship that took a long time to build and to pay off. A good recruiter will stay in touch with you, but that recruiter is more interested in hearing from you periodically. A time may even come when you can reward your friend by passing along a search yourself. Just because you've been placed doesn't mean that your file goes into storage. Although no reputable recruiter is ever going to recruit you away from the client organization where you were placed, the world of employment takes strange turns. Who knows when you may need your hard-earned friend again? Make that *friends*— you will want to keep in touch with all of those on your target list.

Cultivating the right headhunters can be the wisest investment you'll ever make—one that pays dividends for a working lifetime—and costs you nothing more than postage and an occasional phone call.

Mr. Sibbald heads his own Chicago search firm, John Sibbald Associates, and also wrote The New Career Makers, *a book that includes extensive profiles of leading recruiters.*

How to Curry a Headhunter's Favor

by Gabrielle Solomon

When job hunters try to connect with executive recruiters (and vice versa), misunderstandings often follow. That's because many candidates assume—wrongly—that headhunters are supposed to find them new positions. This misconception may lead job seekers to become discouraged by unintended recruiter slights, behave coolly or rudely during telephone screenings or waste precious time on unproductive search activities. As a result, they may miss out on opportunities for which they're well-qualified.

To be sure, search consultants play a key role in the job market, and it's possible to enjoy a mutually beneficial relationship with them. However, recruiters say that first you must realize that they're paid by hiring companies, and that's where their loyalties lie.

"Candidates are not our clients; the company is our client," says Herman DeKesel, managing partner of the Palo Alto, CA, office of TASA International, a retained search firm. "[Still], it's probably good to establish a relationship with recruiters. It helps your networking."

Before you start, understand the difference between contingency and retained search firms. Contingency recruiters work primarily on middle management and professional-level openings, and are paid only if they successfully fill a position. If you have highly marketable skills, they may shop you around to clients in hope that one will hire you and pay their fee. Retained recruiters, on the other hand, typically work on higher-level executive openings, and receive a fee for conducting a thorough search, regardless of whether any of the candidates they locate are hired. Thus, unless you fit one of their assignments exactly, there's no profit motive for retained recruiters to make employers aware of your existence.

Indeed, if you're actively looking for a new position, sending a generic resume to hundreds of recruiting firms—contingency or retained—probably isn't worth the time, search consultants say.

"We get dozens of unsolicited resumes from job hunters each day, but I don't think I've placed more than three or four of them in 15 years," says Mr. DeKesel. "The chances that you'll match [a current senior-management assignment] and happen to be the best candidate for it are very unlikely."

Instead, you're better off conducting an aggressive job campaign in which you target appropriate employers and research their hiring managers' needs. And to make sure all your bases are covered, try to build fruitful, long-term relationships with a few recruiters in your field throughout your career (instead of just when you're job hunting). To do so, heed the following advice from search consultants.

Preparation

1. **Get noticed.** If recruiters never call you even though you're a skilled executive, "you're either not all that good or you're not all that visible," says Jeff Christian, principal of Christian & Timbers Inc., a retained search firm based in Cleveland.

   To appear on headhunters' radar screens, you must be in the right place at the right time, says Richard L. Hardison, managing director in Dallas for the executive recruiting firm Korn/Ferry International. Consultants often work from a target list of 100 to 150 companies that are highly regarded in their industry, and select candidates who occupy conspicuous positions at A-list employers, Mr. Hardison says.

   To increase your chances of attracting a recruiter's attention, try to work more closely with peers and customers and become more active in your company or industry association, Mr. Hardison advises. For example, you might call your company's marketing vice president or public relations director and volunteer your services, says Mr. Christian. Say you're willing to serve as a contact name on press releases and be quoted in trade-journal articles. You might even develop relationships with journalists who cover your industry, or write some essays yourself.

2. **Identify suitable recruiters.** Search consultants say that all resumes sent to their firms are reviewed, and most are entered into a database of candidates that gets checked at the start of each assignment. Rest assured, then, that any firm which has your resume will find it and call you if you fit the qualifications for a position it needs to fill. If you can't abide such a passive approach, research and network to locate recruiters who are more likely to take a special interest in you.

   "If at all possible, try to establish some kind of personal connection with the recruiter," says Dave Hoffmann, CEO of DHR International Inc., a retainer search firm based in Chicago. "We probably get 20 to 25 calls a day from candidates, and it's impossible to respond to all of them. But chances are, I will talk to someone who's unique and has mentioned a personal connection."

For example, try to find out who a firm's clients are, then in your resume or follow-up call, play up the value you could bring one of those employers, Mr. Hoffmann suggests. Even better, seek a referral by asking trusted colleagues or human resources executives ar former employers to tell you which recruiters they work with, says Mr. Christian. If you mention to a recruiter that you're calling at the suggestion of, say, former client Jane Smith, you're much more likely to receive the favor of a substantive conversation. Instead of pushing for job leads, try requesting two minutes of advice on how best to market yourself, Mr. Christian suggests. And keep in mind that recruiters who specialize in your field typically will make themselves more accessible to you.

3. **Create an accomplishments-oriented resume.** Resumes and cover letters you send to recruiters should highlight your achievements in a concise format, says Mr. Hoffmann. Recruiters often are looking for a specific type of experience, but too many job hunters let that information get lost in the shuffle. So instead of relying on "glamour and rhetoric," get right to the point, he says.

"A good resume focuses on your contributions and can easily be read in ten seconds," says Mr. Christian.

That doesn't mean eliminating all detail, however. "I want short and sweet chronologies" that include one or two accomplishments in each position, says David Woo, vice president of the insurance division for Management Recruiters International in New York City. "Bulleted points are fine, but they shouldn't be storybooks. Pique my interest: If I want to know more, I'll pick up the phone and ask."

Also be sure to include your compensation history in your cover letter, Mr. Hoffmann says. Since many clients won't consider candidates who fall outside of their set salary range, recruiters will guess your pay if you don't volunteer the information. And if they make a mistake, you may be excluded unnecessarily.

"We'll make judgments [about salary history] based on a person's title and so on, but we can be wrong about it," Mr. Hoffmann says.

On the Phone

4. **Take the call.** Many candidates eliminate themselves from consideration for promising opportunities by making it difficult for recruiters to reach them. "Some people make themselves inaccessible," says Mr. Har-

dison in Dallas. "Their calls are screened very closely, and some secretaries return mailed information."

Even if you're happy in your current position, hearing a recruiter out will provide you with useful job-market information (e.g., qualities employers are looking for or compensation ranges at other companies), says Mr. Hardison. If you're not interested, say so, but try to help by providing names or information about other executives who might be suitable.

"If you're knowledgeable and friendly, you'll get a check by your name," says Mr. Hardison. "The fact that someone is polite and open reinforces that they're a good person, and in the future, [recruiters] remember those people."

5. **Investigate the firm.** Before spending much time talking with a recruiter, it's wise to make sure he or she is legitimate. So early in the conversation, make an excuse to get off the phone. Before calling back, check a reference, such as the annual *Directory of Executive Recruiters* (Kennedy Publications, Fitzwilliam, NH), to see where the firm has offices and whether it's a member of the Association of Executive Search Consultants, which has an ethics code. When you return the call, consider how professionally the phone is answered and ask how long the firm has been in business.

Consider also who the client company is, advises Mr. DeKesel. Some small, emerging employers in the Silicon Valley, for example, haven't been around long enough to know who the best and most ethical search firms are. If you're wary, ask the recruiter to send you a written copy of the job specifications.

"If it's a good job write-up from a large search firm, the recruiter probably knows what he's doing and it's not a fly-by-night operation," says Mr. DeKesel.

The fear, of course, is that your boss—or the world at large—will find out you're testing the job-search waters. While many recruiters say confidentiality isn't a problem in their industry, others concede that there are good and not-so-good firms.

Contingency recruiters may float your resume around to client companies unless you specifically ask them not to, says Mr. DeKesel. Even then, "some recruiters will respect [confidentiality] more than others," he says.

And while Mr. Woo in New York says he'd never send a resume to a client without getting the candidate's permission first, he's aware of other firms that have done so.

6. **Be candid.** In an initial telephone conversation, recruiters talk in broad strategic terms about an opportunity and where you might fit in. They expect you to do the same.

"Some people are way too premature in describing their whole job history," says Mr. Hardison. "Others launch into a litany of questions that probably aren't germane. It's best to focus on strategic ideas and issues, not on minutiae."

And while it's important to be honest, you don't have to reveal your entire background from the start. "I'd provide the same level of disclosure that the recruiter offers," says Mr. Hardison.

If you're unemployed, though, don't try to hide that fact, says Mr. Hoffmann. "It's always a turnoff if someone tries to disguise his or her current situation," he says. "Ultimately, we'll find out anyway."

Never lie or embellish your background, warns Mr. Hoffmann. When you're discovered, "we'll never deal with you again," he says.

7. **Follow up professionally.** If the first conversation goes well, the recruiter will ask for your resume or CV, and possibly for references, says Mr. Hoffmann. Over a period of about 20 days, the recruiter will narrow the slate of candidates and present the top finalists to the employer. Perhaps five will be invited for in-person interviews. During that time, you may have additional telephone interviews and your references may be checked.

This process can be lengthy, so be patient, recruiters say. Use this time to research the company so you can ask intelligent questions and make sophisticated observations in interviews, says Mr. Christian. And fell free to update the recruiter periodically on your progress during this time. Even if you don't get this job, if you handle yourself professionally, you'll have a friend in the recruiting ranks when you're through.

Gabrielle Solomon is associate editor of the National Business Employment Weekly.

Conventional Retainer Search vs. Contingency Recruiting

Conventional executive recruiters view themselves as professionals and argue that they should be paid whether or not they are successful in filling a position. (Like the doctors who earn fees whether or not the patient dies and lawyers who similarly are paid whether or not successful for their clients). This is called "retainer" or "retained" search. Clients pay a portion of the fee to initiate the search, then most or all of the remainder over the next 60 or 90 days regardless of progress on the search itself.

Contingency search, however, incorporates a different way of charging the hiring organization: no fee is due until the candidate is actually hired.

The Association of Executive Search Consultants goes as far as legally advisable to bar contingency work by its member firms (though the definition of "contingency" gets pretty convoluted at times.)

Contingency recruiters argue that payment for performance is the American Way, and that they are **not** under pressure to submit dozens of candidates or push a particular one to increase chances of a "hit."

Actually, there's something to be said on both sides . . . and **the executive seeking maximum exposure should certainly be in touch with all possible recruiters. Remember that neither conventional nor contingency recruiters ever charge the individual: all fees are assumed by the hiring organization.**

Assessing an Executive Recruiter Who Contacts You

1. Beware of phony firms: never pay any money, not even a "registration" fee. Legitimate recruiters never, but never, charge the individual.
2. Don't expect an instant interview or even super-courteous treatment. Recruiters owe their allegiance—and their time—to the hiring organizations who pay their fees.
3. Ask if the recruiter has a specific assignment or is just fishing ... and act accordingly: A low-level contingency recruiter might be tempted to troll your availability and blow your cover. Retainer recruiters don't "float" resumes.
4. Cover yourself at your present job. Tell your employer from Day 1 that you're frequently called by recruiters and that talking with them doesn't mean you're disloyal. This will give you more flexibility and few sleepless nights when you really are "looking."
5. Don't play games with legitimate recruiters on your career objectives, salary, etc. ... but don't spill your guts to everyone who calls you by phone. It's a good sign if the recruiter wants a personal interview: it's in your best interests to cooperate.
6. You can sometimes judge a book by its cover. Visit the recruiter's office and get brochures, reprints, etc., describing the firm ... and judge for yourself. (Note: too-fancy offices can be a negative signal, too, as hundreds burned by career counselors can attest.)

How to Screen Headhunter Calls

by Robert W. Dingman

Accept calls only from people with search firms you respect or when the recruiter is calling at the suggestion of a valued colleague or peer.

Where the caller's firm is unknown, have these questions ready for use by you or your secretary:

1. Are you a retained or contingency firm?
2. Are you seeking business, conducting a search that you are calling me about or checking a reference?
3. Is your firm a member of the Association of Executive Search Consultants?
4. Could you send me a write-up on your search and some material on your firm before we talk?

Depending on the responses, you will know what to do.

If you know the call is a reference check on a former employee and you want to handle it quickly, be sure to call the firm back so you can be sure who you are talking to. When your response may have some negatives in it, this is an essential precaution.

Why bother to talk to search consultants at all? There are a number of reasons that could make it a good use of your time:

- You may learn of new developments in your industry.
- You will be able to get up-to-date ideas of prevailing compensation rates or how hard it is to find the type of person being sought.
- You may learn of a position that fits a friend or colleague that is looking for a new spot.
- You may find that you are being underpaid for what you are doing.

- You may learn of an impressive search firm that you will want to use in the future.
- The job in question may be a great opportunity for you!

Robert W. Dingman is chairman of Robert W. Dingman Co., an executive search firm in Westlake Village, Calif.

Avoid These Mistakes When Dealing with Your Executive Recruiter

by James H. Kennedy

1. Floating a typeset resume complete with picture and reference quote from Sister Mary Loretta in fifth grade. Keep it simple. A typewritten page or two in standard format is just fine.

2. Phoning: "Did you get my resume?" Even if you're lucky enough to get through to the recruiter, he's immediately sorry he took the call, because he thought it was the other Mr. Barofsky (a current client).

3. Phoning 60 days later: "What's up: got anything for me yet?" Your slim chance of ever getting referred just went down the drain.

4. Saying that Jim Kennedy gave you his name and suggested you write or call. I sell a large number of the Directory of Executive Recruiters, so this ploy doesn't work either.

5. Lying about your age, education, job title, salary, etc. Little White Lies can turn into Big Black Clouds that come back to haunt you, even after hiring!

6. Missing an interview date. Miss your grandmother's funeral if necessary, but never an interview set up by your faithful headhunter . . . because then you're history.

7. Failing to take the recruiter's advice on appropriate dress. White-on-white shirts and Nehru jackets may still be fine in Kankakee, but never on Sunday in Silicon Valley.

8. Refusing to take the recruiter's call after you get the job. Next time you're on the beach he won't return your calls, either!

9. Asking: "What did you think of my resume?" Get advice from your first boss or wife (may be the same person), or from Aunt Alice the English teacher, but don't expect the recruiter to be your personal career counselor.

10. Expecting too much. Remember that the recruiter is paid by the other side and is really interested in you only if you can be converted into a bank deposit. Don't expect him to return your calls or give you an interview (but expose yourself to enough and you'll get some action.)

James H. Kennedy is founder, editor and publisher of Executive Recruiter News.

Why Job-Changers Shouldn't Pester Headhunters

by William G. Hetzel

Executive search professionals appreciate receiving resumes "over the transom," but telephone calls from unknown candidates aren't welcome or necessary.

Rest assured that we scan every incoming resume, keep them on file and review them when we receive new assignments to determine if any candidates "fit" the description. At that time, we'll call you to see if you're interested.

We also may return your phone calls; members of my firm always do. However, telephone conversations from candidates who call to, "Just check to see if you received my resume," are the bane of my professional existence.

This is a practical, not a personal, matter: Recruiters don't have the time to conduct "courtesy" interviews with people they don't know. (However, we may make exceptions for very senior officers of large corporations.)

Most job seekers realize that recruiters can't help them unless they have a suitable assignment. But some otherwise capable professionals are so traumatized by unemployment that they forget this reality. They may even call monthly "just to check . . . ," obviously not recognizing that this immediately puts them in our "never-consider" file. As one colleague puts it, "If the Lord himself asks for help finding a new position, and I don't have an assignment for a Lord, there's nothing I can do to help."

People assume that executive recruiters are aware of all kinds of job openings. Not true. We only know about our current assignments, and a few others we may have discussed with clients. Typically, we don't share information about our searches with other recruiters. Consequently, candidates who are expert networkers may know of more job opportunities than we do!

Now, if I already know you, it's a different story. Perhaps I called you in the past and you were courteous and helpful. Possibly we were introduced by a mutual friend. Making this connection requires networking, which is harder and often seems self-serving when you're unemployed. Perhaps the moral is: When employed, nurture your network.

William G. Hetzel is president of The Hetzel Group, an Inverness, IL executive search firm.

This article is reprinted by permission of the *National Business Employment Weekly,* copyright © 1996, Dow Jones & Co., Inc., 1996. All rights reserved. For subscription information, call 800-JOB-HUNT.

What You as a Candidate Should Know

by Robert W. Dingman

You have indicated an interest in discussing a position we are seeking to fill for a client firm. That makes you a "candidate" in the lexicon of the search consultant. Let's clarify what this process entails and what you can expect from us (and from all ethical recruiters). This explanation is intended to provide information of our responsibility to both you and your client. We would not want you to be confused about what comes next.

First, we are retained by the client firm, never paid by a candidate, on only a retainer-fee basis versus a contingent-fee arrangement. We will be paid whether or not you or the other candidates are hired. Consequently, even though you are a candidate We are not primarily serving your interests. Even if we may believe you are "perfect" for the position we are discussing, We have a responsibility to our client to present a panel of well-qualified candidates; so you will have a built-in competition from our efforts. Overwhelmingly, our search assignments are successfully completed, so there are minimal financial reasons for us to pressure you or the client to make a match. Lastly, like most search firms, our fees are usually based on a percentage of the first year's cash compensation of the person selected. This means that if you were able to negotiate a higher figure with our client, it is to our financial advantage, but you should know that we will never assist you to raise that amount. If the client requests it, we will serve as an intermediary in salary negotiations, but our function is only to help reduce communication problems.

If we request references from you, there are things you should know about what will ensue. We do not want references who are likely to let the word out that you are being considered for a position and then have this complicate your current work situation. The worst professional blunder we can make is to be indiscreet and compromise your employment somehow. We take this responsibility very seriously, so please give us names of people who will be discreet. Because we are a one-office firm, reference material does not go to other offices. The less circulated information is the more likely that confidentiality is maintained.

Why do we need to check references, anyhow? The knowledge we gain is essential if both your interests and those of the client are to be served well, and reference checking is that tool for gathering that information. Neither we, nor anyone, has the ability on the basis of an interview alone to know fully the strengths and limitations of an executive.

Ideally, we like to get views of a candidate from superiors, peers and subordinates. If we continue our discussions to the point where you are a "finalist" whom we present to the client, we will at some point feel free to discreetly contact references other than the ones you named. Our responsibility to our client requires that we document your achievements. It is professionally embarrassing for us to have a client encounter a candidate misstatement, whether it involves compensation, professional achievements, reason for termination, pertinent personal data, degrees or employment dates. Material misrepresentations make it very difficult for us to present such a candidate because of concern about veracity.

A last comment on referencing. You will never hear from us what your references said about you. The data we collect is sacrosanct and is shared only with the client, *if* we present you. Naturally, if we present you as a finalist your references must have, on balance, been supportive of you. Conversely, if you are *not* presented it would be unwise to assume that it was due to poor references because so many other factors are involved.

We will be as candid with you in our dealings as the situation allows. If our candor is sometimes at the expense of being sensitive and tactful, please forgive us. We will not string you along if things are not going to move forward. You have honored us with your time and interest, and candor is the very least we owe you. When the search is completed, we will let you know who was selected. If the client met you and you were not selected, we will feed back to you any information that we are free to share that might be useful to you in future interviews.

Each of us has only one career, and a mistake in changing jobs can prove disruptive and harmful. We covenant with you that if we get to the "short strokes" with a client, we will tell you all the negatives we know about the client organization and personnel, as well as the positive things that recruiters always point out. We take seriously the responsibility of possibly shaping the future direction of your career.

If any of these comments raises questions for you, or something is not acceptable to you in what we have spelled out, let's discuss it. Please excuse us if this sounds formidable, because it really isn't and perhaps you understood how it all works. However, not everyone does and it is important for every candidate to be fully informed.

Robert W. Dingman of Robert W. Dingman Co., Westlake Village, Calif., wrote this and gives a copy to every candidate.

The Seven Most Common Blunders Made by Executives on Their Resumes and Cover Letters

1. **Don't be informal.** Don't start your cover letter with the words: "Good morning" or "How are you today?" Don't address the executive recruiter by his or her first name in your letter. Don't begin your letter with "Can we talk?"

2. **Don't use colored paper** such as chartreuse, orange, brown or gray. Besides giving the wrong impression, they don't xerox well and sooner or later, your resume, if it is of interest to a company, will have to be copied.

3. **Don't include a picture.** In the '40s or '50s, this practice was popular. Today, it's passe and gives the impression that you're old-fashioned. In any case, please don't send an 8½ by 11 glossy. Even if you have movie star good looks, it has little impact on the search firm in determining your suitability for a job.

4. **Don't use gimmicks.** While they work well for people looking for jobs in the advertising industry, they work against you for corporate posts. Don't tape a nickel or a dollar bill on your cover letter; don't send your resume in a file folder labeled with your name.

5. **Watch your language.** Don't start your cover letter with a bang, i.e., "Are you looking for a marketing superstar?" It's better to err on the boring side than to be too promotional. Don't hype your letter with terms like, "I'm a young 57" or "I'm a high-powered executive."

6. **Leave out personal information.** No one is interested in your wife's maiden name (unless it's DuPont), your children's names and ages, when you graduated high school, or your religion.

7. **Don't send too much material.** Don't send your present company's annual report; don't turn your resume into a book-length project and don't send references. If a search firm or other employer needs that sort of back-up, you're probably on the verge of getting the job.

Source: Battalia Winston Int'l. Inc., a New York-based executive search firm that is a member of the Euram Consultants Group, Ltd., with offices throughout Europe.

Save Time:
Do It Right the First Time!

by Chuck Brooks

When you fail to include key information with your resume, you run the risk of getting the whole thing tossed, or put into a dead-end file or pile, or requiring a lot of mail/phone/fax follow up.

ALWAYS BE SURE TO SUPPLY RECRUITERS WITH THE FOLLOWING INFORMATION WHEN YOU SEND IN YOUR RESUME:

1. Present or most recent *compensation* (including breakdown if more than straight salary)
2. The *minimum* compensation you would consider
3. Your *relocation* preferences or restrictions, if any

Chuck Brooks is a recruiter with Executives' Personnel Service, Inc. in Southfield, Mich.

Some Thoughts on Resumes

A resume is as essential to a job search as wings are to a bird: it's impossible to fly without it. But whether you call it an essential evil or whatever, it must be a mirror image (albeit a bit polished) of its subject. Embellishment leads to jail (or at least disappointment): shyness or sloppiness errs in the other direction.

Show me a person who can't distill a lifetime onto two pages and I'll show you a scatterbrain or an egomaniac.

Printers' resumes—and maybe a few others in the creative arena—are appropriately printed. For all the rest, neat typing does it.

COMMENT: A resume is like a snowflake: highly individualized & painfully short-lived . . . but best used in large quantities. The statistical chances of a few resumes producing results are so miniscule as to justify mass distribution to all likely targets, in most cases.

Five Steps to Evaluate a Job Offer Before Accepting

by James H. Lane

Employers shouldn't be the only ones asking for references during the job hunting process.

Job candidates should carefully evaluate the "credentials" of prospective employers as well.

Too many employment disasters occur because individuals do not do their homework before accepting a new position. When a company makes a job offer, there's risk on both sides, but it's far greater for the candidate than for the company, especially if the position involves relocation.

To avoid taking the wrong career step, job candidates should research five key areas before saying "yes":

1. **Talk with Current Employees.** Try to meet employees at all levels: your peers, prospective boss, and subordinates. Make a special effort to spend ample time with the boss, in a social environment as well as in the office. The higher the job level, the more important the "chemistry" and the more subjective the hiring process.

2. **Check Customer References.** Don't be shy quizzing customers about their satisfaction with the company's product or service; why they selected the firm as a vendor; strengths and weakness from a customer's perspective; as well as projections about their business relationship in the future.

3. **Financial Stability of the Company.** If the firm is publicly held, the company should be willing to provide certain information at your request. Depending on the seniority of the position, it may be advisable to get a professional financial opinion, especially in the case of a privately owned operation. Other good sources of financial information include investors, whether venture capital or banks, and vendors. (If they don't pay on time, there's a good chance your paychecks may not be predictable!)

4. **The Work Environment.** Make sure you see where you'll be working and get a clear picture of the available resources, including the professional/clerical support necessary to do the job.
5. **Organizational Expectations.** Understanding and adapting to the "corporate culture" is critical, especially at executive levels. The new boss management style, level of expectations and communications approach will be important factors in determining your success on the job.

Don't overlook these points, but remember to sell yourself first, get the offer, and THEN ask the tough questions.

For individuals who find themselves in a new situation that looks like a mismatch, start looking immediately. The longer you stay in the "wrong" job, the more you damage your employment credentials. A brief stay with a company is easier to explain in your next interview than a series of one or two-year stints.

James H. Lane wrote this while he was with Costello & Company, an outplacement firm in Norwell, Mass. He is currently a principal in another firm, Lane, Gaffney & Co., in Concord, Mass.

Things Your Headhunter Won't Tell You . . .

Ethical recruiters (and most are, by the way) recognize their responsibility to candidates as well as to the hiring organization and share as much information as possible about the position and the search process. Regrettably, however, sometimes communications break down because of neglect or nefariousness: you've got to be prepared for these eventualities as well.

Advice to candidates

Item	Explanation
We're quoting $150K, but they'll go to $200K if necessary.	You can't blame your new employer for wanting to get you for as small a compensation package as you feel comfortable accepting. Besides, this gives them more space for a raise if you perform well.
The last guy (person) in this job quit because he couldn't get along with the founder's son, who's exec vp.	Blood is thicker than water, and nepotism is king at this place, but if you can stick it out for a few years and negotiate a fat contract you'll still be ahead of the game.
You're the first candidate we're recommending here, mainly to test our understanding of the specs.	Somebody's got to be the walking horse, somebody's got to be first. Look at it this way: early bird gets the worm (sometimes).
As a woman, you don't have much of a chance to get this job, but the client wants to be covered on EEO.	If it's any consolation to you, we're also throwing in a black and a guy with a limp.
The real reason we couldn't recommend you was those long sideburns and white socks.	Remember, this was for McKinsey & Co., not your everyday software house.

Too bad we didn't have a picture before calling you in for this interview.	Otherwise we'd have known you're a black female and would have gotten you in earlier in anticipation of scoring two points on our client's EEO scale.
You're perfect for the job, but I can only use you as a source because we already have the search to find your company's new CEO.	Even headhunters follow the rules of the jungle.

The Lexicon of Executive Recruiting

A Glossary of Terms Used in the Professional Process of Searching for Executives

Compiled and published by *Executive Recruiter News,* the independent newsletter of the executive search profession.

Annual Retainer.   A form of volume discounting of executive search services. Client agrees to pay so much a month, quarter or year, thereby establishing a credit account against which specific placements are billed. Encourages long-term relationships for greater efficiency, lower marketing costs, improved client service.

Appraisal Interview.   See EVALUATION OF CANDIDATES.

Association of Executive Search Consultants (AESC).   Organized in 1959 as the Association of Executive Recruiting Consultants, Inc., this association brought together leading executive search consultants who established strict requirements for membership and standards of ethical practice for their professional field. AESC membership identifies the consultant who is not only pledged to these high standards but who is also accredited by his professional peers to conduct his practice with professional competence and integrity. (See page 146 for address.)

Blockages.   Places where recruiters cannot look for candidates to fill a position. Usually refers to corporations that are off-limits because they are, or recently have been, clients of the search firm (see Off Limits Policy).

Body-Snatcher.   See HEADHUNTER.

Boutique. An executive search firm that specializes in one or more relatively narrow niches in contrast to presenting a generalist image.

Bundling. Relatively new term describing the talents required in today's "super executive" who is brought in to replace two or three others and is expected to reflect a "bundling" of all their attributes. Bad for search in that there are fewer jobs to fill, but good because super-execs are scarce & hard to find, requiring professional search.

Candidate. A person who survives extensive screening, reference-checking and interviewing and is to be presented to the client for the position to be filled.

Candidate Blockages. Candidates who may not be considered for a position because they are active candidates in another search.

Candidate Reports. Summaries prepared on each final candidate that usually include a complete employment history, personal biographical data, appraisal of qualifications, and initial reference information. Data is verified and submitted to the client for examination prior to the first meeting with the candidate. Where possible, search consultants prefer to make their presentation in person so as to permit maximum exchange of ideas and information.

Career Counselors. Firms or individuals offering services to individuals. Some are legitimate but many are not. Some have been forced out of business by state Attorneys General for failure to meet promises: many have been investigated. (Be wary of claims in blaring ads in Wall Street Journal, N.Y. Times, etc.) Services can include psychological testing, resume preparation, interview training, job-search planning, etc. Fees can run from modest to $10,000! Read fine print in contracts and check with legal counsel before making a down payment or signing anything. Dealing with a small, local counselor on a 1-1 basis is usually best and least expensive. Extreme caution is advised.

Client. Organization sponsoring and paying the recruiter for a search.

Client Anonymity. One of the principal reasons for using executive search. Client identity is usually not revealed to prospective candidates until well along in the process, except in general terms.

Client Block. See OFF LIMITS POLICY.

Code of Ethics. Every profession has found it necessary to establish a code of ethics as a necessary part of the process of self-discipline, and to protect the interests of clients and assure them of fair treatment. A code of professional ethics helps the practitioner determine the propriety of his conduct in his professional relationships. It indicates the kind of professional posture the practitioner must develop and maintain if he is to succeed. It gives the clients and potential clients a basis for feeling confident that the professional person desires to serve them well, and places services ahead of financial reward. It gives clients assurance that the professional person will do his work in conformity with professional standards of competence, independence and integrity. The AESC Code of Ethics is followed by many executive recruiting consultants in North America.

Compensation Package.   Total compensation can include various elements other than salary for senior executives: typically a mix of deferred income, incentive bonus, profit-sharing, stock options, tax shelters (or some type of compensation that permits estate-building), thrift plans, pension plans, life insurance, health insurance, long-term disability insurance, dental insurance, tuition assistance, payment for personal and family medical and dental expenses, cars, club memberships, loans, joining bonus and other perquisites (including, increasingly, some form of hiring bonus).

Completion Rate.   Percentage of retained searches that result in a hire. Estimated to be as low as 60%, claimed by some to be 100% (be wary of the latter: no one is perfect, and the imponderables/intangibles in a search are many). Greatly affected by client lassitude in interviewing and following up with candidates, changes (written and subtle) in job specifications, internal client politics, organizational changes, etc. . . . as well as by recruiter performance and effectiveness.

Confidential Search.   There are times when it is important for the client to conduct confidential searches. When secrecy is necessary, it is virtually impossible to handle a search from within the organization. For example, a company may want to introduce a whole new line of products or acquire a new product or company before competitors learn about it. In such cases, a recruiter can work effectively on its behalf without disclosing its identity until the final stages of the search. The company can make its selection and announce its plans after the new executive is on board.

Keeping a search totally confidential requires considerable discipline and skill on the part of both client and recruiter. Once the client has been identified to the top two or three candidates, both the client and the recruiter must be ready and able to move fast to make a final decision and a public announcement. This is the only way to avoid possible leaks, and it requires careful coordination.

"Con-tainer" Search.   Fee arrangement that combines elements of retainer and contingency methods of payment. Usually involves an initiation payment and progress payment(s) that may not be refundable, with a "success" or "completion" portion due only on actual hiring.

Contingency Search.
The search consultant who uses the contingent fee approach must fill the position before his fee is paid by the client, and this can change the entire rationale of the assignment.

There is a strong tendency for some recruiters who conduct contingency searches to spend as little time as possible on a search, to refer as many candidates as possible, or to compromise standards by referring mediocre or marginal candidates to the client.

On the other hand, a minority of contingency recruiters visit their clients, interview their candidates, conduct reference checks and otherwise differ from their retainer counterparts only in mechanics of payment.

Dehiring.
See OUTPLACEMENT.

Directory of Executive Recruiters.
Listing published by Kennedy Publications since 1971. Thousands of names and addresses, with salary minimums and areas of specialty (indexed by management function, industry and geography). Updated annually.

Employment Agency.
Employment agencies normally limit their efforts to representing individuals who are actively looking for new employment opportunities within the local area. When an organization contacts an agency to fill a specific job opening, the agency usually reviews its files for applications from people with appropriate backgrounds and may place ads in local newspapers to attract additional applicants.

Employment agencies often try to place their applicants in any of a large number of local organizations because they are paid by the individual applicant or employer only if a placement is made. They make the majority of their placements in the lower salary ranges. Their payment is a fee based on the employee's starting salary.

Their fees may be regulated by the state and frequently follow the pattern of a 5 percent minimum plus 1 percent for each $1,000 of the annual salary of the individual employed, up to a maximum of 20-30 percent. Some states also permit an advance fee or charge to the individual who lists himself with an employment agency. The line between Fee Paid Employment Agency and Contingency Recruiter is sometimes very difficult to draw.

Employment Agreement.
When the client organization and candidate have agreed on terms of employment, it is usually important to put these into writing as a protection to both parties. The employment agreement may take the

form of a formal agreement or letter to the new executive spelling out everything discussed and agreed upon: job specifications, reporting relationships, base salary, benefits, moving costs, etc. The executive will then reply, either by telephone or letter, and the deal will be settled.

Equal Opportunity Act. An Equal Employment Opportunity Commission was established in Washington, D.C. in 1964 to prevent employment discrimination. (The Roosevelt Administration established a similar organization to prevent such discrimination during World War II.) Although the law demands that women and other minority employees be considered for executive positions at various levels, most organizations, for example, lack candidates with both the education and experience required for such positions. Consequently, a growing number of these organizations must look outside for qualified individuals from the relatively small pool of qualified middle and top managers. To help such companies, some search firms have set up special departments to recruit such executives. Others specialize in this field.

Evaluation of Candidates. At a convenient time and place, the recruiter interviews the prospective candidate to verify the original information gathered during the process of sourcing and researching, to examine his background in depth, and to determine if the personal chemistry will be appropriate.

These appraisal interviews develop an in-depth picture of each candidate: his employment background, business philosophy, career objectives, potential and personality characteristics. Education and employment are verified, and a reference investigation is made of past performance. From the group of prospective candidates evaluated, several of the best-qualified are selected for introduction to the client. During this phase of an engagement, the recruiter's breadth of background, depth of insight and sound judgment are critical.

Evaluation of Executive Recruiter. What benchmarks should the client use in evaluating the recruiter's performance over a period of time? They include professionalism, results, adequate communications, realistic costs, proper staffing of assignments and timing of assignments.

Executive Assimilation Process. The process of integrating the new executive into the organization. See SHAKEDOWN EXERCISE.

Executive Clearing House. These are information centers whose basic function is to bring together employers and candidates for positions on an informational basis. They collect information from two sources: individuals interested in a position, and employers or their search consultants seeking executives to fill specific positions. The information concerning the person and the position is classified and put into a mechanized or computerized retrieval system. Both the individual and the employer are expected to share the cost of these information centers. Companies may pay either a standard amount per position or per year, or a placement fee if and when they employ a person referred by the Clearing House. Some of these have been computerized into Job Banks or Registries of one sort or another. Caution is advised.

Executive Recruiting.   The service performed for a fee by independent and objective persons or a group of consultants organized as a firm or similar entity. Executive recruiters help managers of client organizations identify and appraise executives well-qualified to fill specific management positions in commerce, industry, government, and the nonprofit field. Their fees are paid by the organizations that retain them.

This highly specialized area of the management consulting profession started as a normal service rendered by general management consulting firms. Executive recruiting has experienced rapid growth since the end of World War II, both in the United States and abroad. There are hundreds of consultants (most of whom refer to themselves as "firms") that handle executive search either as a specialty or in conjunction with other forms of consulting work.

Executive recruiting firms, also known as executive search consultants, generally bill their clients monthly as the search progresses and deduct these payments from the total fee, frequently up to 35 percent of the first year's total compensation. Some may use other methods of billing such as a regular per diem, or a flat fee, plus out-of-pocket expenses.

The true role of the executive recruiting consultant is not that of a glorified pirate, body-snatcher, headhunter, or any other erroneous label frequently applied to him or her.

Executive recruiting consultants are usually willing to receive resumes from executives seeking new job opportunities, but they are not in a position to help executives find jobs.

Executive Referral.   Euphemism for RESUME FLOATING to former or present client.

Executive Search.   Synonym for EXECUTIVE RECRUITING, although some feel strongly that "search" better describes the process and identifies its major thrust.

Expenses.   Additions to the search fee intended to compensate the recruiter for out-of-pocket payments incurred specifically for a given search (i.e. telephone calls, special directories or subscriptions, candidate & recruiter travel, etc). An item to be carefully monitored by the diligent client, as some search firms tend to "make money" on expenses (double-billing for travel involving two clients, for example). Other firms attempt to recover ordinary administrative expenses. A variable item on the search firm's invoice, but bears watching & documentation of over 15-20% of the fee.

Fair Credit Reporting Acts. Legislation to amend general business law regarding procedures for securing information about individuals seeking commercial credit, loans, jobs, etc. Also covers the confidentiality, accuracy, relevancy and proper use of such information. Can affect the reference-checking aspect of executive recruiting significantly. Regulations vary widely from state to state.

Fallout. Term popularly used to describe the following condition: after a placement has been made (or during the assignment), the client decides to hire one or more additional candidates who surfaced and were recommended by the recruiter. Some search firms demand full fee for each such additional hire: others will not accept a fee. Most frequently a matter of negotiation dependent on the time frame, client relations, etc. See PLACEMENT, MULTIPLE.

Fee. The total fee paid by the client to an executive recruiter for a search assignment. Most recruiters these days charge clients 30-33 percent of the first year's total compensation for the executive hired, plus out-of-pocket expenses. Thus, if the new executive is paid $50,000 base salary and no bonus or incentive, the client's fee would be about $15,000 regardless of the billing method, plus 10 to 25 percent of the professional fee for out-of-pocket expenses. Retainer recruiters are paid for their services whether or not a placement is made. See METHODS OF BILLING, FRONT END RETAINER, INVOICING ARRANGEMENT and REIMBURSABLE EXPENSES.

Front-End Retainer. During the course of a search, clients are invoiced monthly for agreed-upon fees, plus out-of-pocket expenses. These monthly installments generally range from one-third to one-fourth of the total fee involved. They are sometimes called "front-end retainers" and are credited toward the total fee when the individual is employed. Usually a final billing for any remaining fee is rendered at that time. Retainer recruiters require a payment before commencing a search. This is also called a "front-end retainer."

Greenlighting. When companies merge, this is the signal given to the manager to start looking, because his counterpart in the other company will assume his role for the combined firm.

Guarantee. Promise by the search firm to replace a failed candidate within a certain period of time (usually one year), especially if caused by negligence on the recruiter's part. Search is usually reinstated for expenses only.

Handwriting Analysis. (Graphology) A controversial selection technique pioneered in Germany and in occasional use elsewhere as another tool to help predict candidate performance and fit.

Headhunter. Formerly pejorative term for executive recruiter, still only passively accepted by professionals in the field . . . currently used more in a jocular and light-hearted sense than critically . . . even voiced occasionally by some headhunters themselves! (Other labels, far less in evidence today, have included "body-snatcher," "pirate," etc.)

Hiring Bonus. A one-time payment originally intended to compensate a joining executive for extra expenses occasioned by a major move. Now viewed somewhat more broadly, though not quite like a professional ball-player "signing bonus," nonetheless the comparison had been made! The concept includes, for example, recompense for "lost" bonuses at the company the executive is leaving. It can also be a device to compensate for lower salary scales in the hiring company. A hiring or joining bonus, then, is whatever it takes in addition to total compensation to convince the candidate to join. The amount can range from a few thousand to over a million dollars, sometimes paid half on joining and half six months later.

Interview. Another word for both preliminary and appraisal interviews which are conducted for the purpose of assessing prospective candidates.

Interview, Stress. This is a Nazi-like technique once promoted by a recruiter in New York City as applicable in executive recruiting. Through it, the prospective candidate is bludgeoned with insulting remarks until he finally loses his temper, thus presumably revealing his true inner self. Few (if any) recruiters use such techniques.

Invoicing Arrangement. Regardless of the type of fee structure used by the recruiter, the client should understand the invoicing arrangement in advance. Many recruiters require a payment before commencing the search. Others will do much of the preliminary work involved in a search before sending the first invoice. Invoices for professional fees and out-of-pocket expenses may be payable monthly for three to four months or may require payment at certain periods during the search, usually with the final payment upon completion of the search.

Job Counselors. See CAREER COUNSELORS and OUTPLACEMENT.

Job Description. This describes the client position to be filled and outlines the desired characteristics and experience that the executive being sought should possess. When approved by the client, the "specs" become the guidelines for the search.

Leaving Money on the Table.   Outside search consultant's lament when placed executive gets higher first-year compensation than was estimated and fee was fixed, not percentage.

Length of Recruiting Assignment.   The average recruiting assignment takes three to four months from the initial meeting with the client until the candidate is finally selected. Once a new executive is selected, it may take two to four weeks or more before he or she actually reports to work. An assignment may take as little as a month or two if everything goes right, but this is rare. On the other hand, a search may take six months to a year. When it lasts that long, chances are that the position was impossible to fill, the specifications were changed, the client was not available to meet candidates or didn't really want to fill the position, the recruiter miscalculated, or something else out of the ordinary happened.

Licensing.   Many years ago, when immigrant laborers were taken advantage of by unethical employment agencies, most states enacted legislation to protect individuals by licensing and control of such agencies. Thus employment agencies are licensed today; executive recruiters are generally not. As employment agencies move into fee-paid and retainer work, the line becomes more difficult to draw. Many states now write specific exemptions for executive recruiters, citing salary minimums and the fact that the individual does not pay a fee.

Lobbing.   Following a shootout, the losing firm "lobs" a resume to the client, showing the kind of candidate the losing firm would have recruited had it been given the assignment.

Methods of Billing.   The most commonly used methods of calculating the professional fees charged for executive search services are:

- A fixed percentage fee, usually 30 to 33 percent of the first year's agreed-upon total compensation of the executive recruited.
- A flat fee, fixed in advance on the basis of estimated time and difficulty of the search.
- A retainer fee for professional services over a stated period of time.
- A straight time formula, based on actual time spent on the search, but sometimes governed by an agreed-to-maximum.
- A per-diem or hourly fee for any candidate appraised and recommended by the recruiter and hired by the client.

In addition to the fee, there are also expenses. These are mainly for travel and communications, and they will vary, depending on the complexity of the search and the distances between client, recruiter and candidates. It is customary for clients to pay for candidates' travel to interviews. See FEE and REIMBURS-ABLE EXPENSES.

Off Limits Policy.   A key issue in executive search. Refers to the recruiter agreeing not to approach executives in the client organization. Factors are definition of "client" and time: the whole corporation (e.g., General Motors) or the division the search was done for (Chevrolet), or some even more specific entity (Truck Division, Northeast Region) . . . and for one year, two, three?

Some large firms say they can't "afford" a strict Off Limits policy because it reduces the universe from which they can draw and gets extremely complicated ("client" served by the San Francisco or Zurich office, how significant a client, etc.). Small firms magnanimously offer "full" worldwide client protection because it doesn't really affect their business.

Whether this is an ethical or trade practice or business issue, it is extremely important to have it fully and mutually understood, preferably in writing, at the outset of a search assignment.

Outplacement.   When executives are fired or dropped by various kinds of organizations today, they are often referred to outplacement consultants. These specialized consultants analyze their abilities and counsel them on how to prepare resumes and find new careers. Outplacement consultants work for and are always paid by the firing organization. A few serve both companies and displaced executives, and there is in such circumstances a potential conflict of interest. The Association of Executive Search Consultants (AESC) bars its members from offering outplacement services for the same reason.

Person Specification.   A synonym for JOB DESCRIPTION.

Personal Chemistry.   There is a rough analogy between mixing chemicals and mixing executives at the top level. By combining executives, an organization can achieve synergy, or neutralization, or can produce explosions. The daily newspapers verify this chemical analogy as it operates in the executive suite.

The search for a new executive is part of a process of organization change, often with traumatic implications. Preparing for this change and tackling the inherent integration problems are essential if the needs of the individual and group are to be met.

In their evaluation of prospective candidates, professional recruiters try hard to determine whether the personal chemistry will be appropriate. A few recruiters help clients integrate new executives into the organization on as firm a footing as possible by means of formal programs. Interpersonal breakdowns can create enormous organizational cost, and it is important to anticipate and head them off.

Pirate.   See HEADHUNTER.

Placement.   The act of an executive recruiter in filling a client position.

Placement, Multiple.   When a recruiter is searching for a top-level executive, he or she frequently interviews candidates who are not exactly right for the position, but who may be of interest to the client for another position. When the client fills a secondary opening with a candidate presented to him for the primary position, it is called a secondary or multiple placement. This happens often enough so that the recruiter should spell out the details in his confirmation letter before commencing the search. Some recruiters charge a full fee; others reduce their fee for a secondary placement because their research effort time devoted to the placement has been absorbed by the primary search. See FALLOUT.

Privacy.   An infrequently used synonym for confidential search. It is also used to refer to the various privacy acts and legislation protecting the individual.

Professional Practice Guidelines.   These are standards of good practice for the guidance of executive recruiters. They make for equitable and satisfactory client relationships and contribute to success in recruiting. (See the AESC Code of Ethics and Professional Practice Guidelines for specific standards of good practice.)

Progress Payments.   Monthly payments made to the recruiter by the client for agreed-upon fees, plus out-of-pocket expenses, during the course of the search. Frequently cited as a key difference between Contingency and Retainer Search.

Proposals, Letters of Agreement and Contracts.   Each recruiting assignment should have as its base point a formal written instrument (usually a letter of agreement or proposal) between the recruiter and the client. It should accurately describe the terms of the assignment. Unwritten agreements often lead to misunderstandings and dissatisfaction on the part of one or both of the parties. The written agreement should be specific on all pertinent points: job or position specifications, responsibilities of each party, amount of fee, method of payment, time limits involved and any other pertinent points of agreement.

Psychological Testing.   Professional search consultants develop their own evaluation methods. Formal psychological evaluation is almost always left to the client's discretion. If a client has doubts about the fitness of a candidate, psychological evaluation may be indicated. But it is not likely that the search consultant will use psychological testing as part of its own selection process.

Ratcheting.   The temptation faced by retainer recruiters charging on a percentage basis: the higher the salary at which the candidate is hired, the higher the fee (even a hint of conflict of interest in such instances is eliminated when charged on fixed-fee basis).

Records Maintenance.   Professional recruiters have clear policies known to their staffs regarding the retention of records and coding in compliance with existing laws and regulations on federal and state levels, together with the spirit of the various privacy acts and legislation protecting the individual.

Recruiting Costs.   See FEE and METHODS OF BILLING.

Recruitment Advertising.   Professional recruiters feel that advertising with regard to a particular assignment should be done judiciously, and only with the approval of the client. It should state the position clearly and be used with discretion. Absolute honesty in statements and actions should be observed in the text of the advertisement.

In Europe and Canada, advertising is commonly used in the executive search process. Sometimes this is called Executive Selection; at other times the terms are interchangeable.

References.   Persons to whom a recruiter refers for testimony as to a candidate's character, background, abilities, etc.

Executive recruiters usually take references proffered by candidates only as a starting point. They then confidentially seek out former superiors, subordinates, peers, colleagues, vendors, suppliers, etc., to get an independent and objective evaluation of the candidate. See below.

Reference Checking.   After intensive interviews with the candidates (but before introduction to the client) the recruiter will begin to check references. Initially the recruiter will be limited to references provided by the candidates. These are likely to be favorable. However, from these references the recruiter will obtain others (known in recruiting as second-generation references) who will be likely to provide a more objective picture of the candidates. These references include such persons as social contacts, professors, business associates and former roommates.

This initial checking of references is a delicate area and must be done with prudence. It is vital that the candidate not be embarrassed or have his current job jeopardized as a result of these checks. In addition, the client often wants the search to remain confidential at this stage.

For these reasons, it is customary to defer an in-depth development of reference information until mutuality of interest has been determined.

Reference investigation and reporting should be conducted with the candidate's prior knowledge; within the spirit and intent of applicable federal and/or state laws and regulations; with persons considered knowledgeable about the candidate and whose information can be cross-checked for objectivity and reliability; and with respect for the personal and professional privacy of all parties concerned. References today are rarely in writing, usually in the form of telephone notes.

Referral Service. Most large banks in metropolitan areas provide a referral service for executives, especially in financial and general management fields. They provide this service at no cost to their customers, and the executives are generally seeking a new position. Often, banks will recommend executives for senior positions if their particular skills will strengthen the customer's position. Large law firms sometimes provide a referral service to their clients. Trade associations and professional organizations also refer names of members who are actively in the job market at no cost to job seekers or interested companies. In addition, placement offices of most universities offer a free referral service, and many graduate schools of business help place their alumni.

Reimbursable Expenses. All recruiters incur out-of-pocket expenses in their day-to-day search activities. Typically, there are travel expenses for both recruiter and candidate, related costs for hotels, meals, long-distance telephone calls, printing and other related costs. Some recruiters charge for their reimbursable expenses at cost while others may add a service charge. Some charge for secretarial, research and other support services while other recruiters absorb part or all of the expenses.

Reimbursable expenses may run from 10 percent to 25 percent of the professional fee or more, depending on such factors as length of assignment, location of client and the majority of candidates, number of offices used by the recruiter and salary range of the position being filled. International searches covering several countries obviously incur higher expenses.

Replacement Guarantee. See GUARANTEE.

Research. The foundation of professional recruiting is research. All well-established recruiting consultants maintain research facilities to develop background information about industries, companies, and key executives. In a rapidly changing business environment, constant research is the principal guarantee against superficial or haphazard research work.

Resource.   Someone who can possibly recommend a candidate for a specific opening.

Resume.   A brief account of personal and educational experience and qualifications of a job applicant. The resume is the first formal contact between a company and a potential employee, and in some ways it is the most critical. Personnel officers in most major corporations can usually give only 20 to 30 seconds of attention for each of the many resumes they see every day. So, to make the best impression, an applicant's resume must be constructed in such a way that it provides the most pertinent information about him or her in the simplest and most easily digestible form. The information should be brief, complete & easily accessible.

Resume Floating.   Frowned-upon practice of sending resumes to a potential hiring organization without a contractual search assignment, in hope of a "hit" ... banned by AESC as "inappropriate."

Retained Search.   Retained search is one in which a client retains a recruiter to identify and appraise executives well-qualified to fill a specific management position. An initial down payment is followed by progress payments, and the full fee may have been paid before the position is actually filled.

Retainer.   A retainer fee (usually paid monthly) for professional services for an agreed-upon period of time.

Rusing.   Using subterfuge to obtain information, typically posing as editor or researcher or personal friend to get information on executive names, titles, etc., in research phase, banned by AESC as unethical. See UNETHICAL RESEARCH.

Search Process, The.   The task of identifying and appraising well-qualified executives is painstaking and time-consuming and must be governed by an orderly approach, consisting of several major steps or phases, if it is to be successful. These steps represent the broad phases of a typical search assignment and identify the major areas of activity involved in the work that recruiters do for clients.

These steps are interrelated and interdependent, but they are often adapted and modified by search consultants as they work out their own approaches to client engagements. The professional search process does not depend on luck, shortcuts, or gimmicks, but on a step-by-step procedure whereby a list of potentially suitable executives is reduced to several uniquely qualified candidates. In outline form, the successful search consultant must: meet with the client to discuss the engagement in depth; develop a strategy or search plan; review files and previous search assignments; contact candidates and evaluate them; check references and participate in negotiations; and follow-up with the client and executive to see how things are going.

The aim is not merely to produce qualified candidates (which is relatively easy) but the very best candidates available.

Second Generation Reference. See REFERENCE CHECKING.

Shakedown Exercise. This exercise or process sometimes involves getting the new executive and his or her boss together in a one- or two-day session with a behavioral psychologist before the new executive reports to work. It is based on the premise that the end of the search process is only the beginning of the more rigorous, more critical process of integration into the new organization. In these sessions, each nails down precisely what each is expecting of the other. The purpose of the shakedown exercise is to bridge the gap between promise and performance. This approach, with its emphasis on behavioral science techniques, is not yet common practice in recruiting.

Shootout. Popular term for competition that finds several search firms making new-business presentations to a potential client. Increasingly used, to the recruiter's chagrin, by sophisticated, cost-conscious or short-sighted clients who sometimes fail to see the value in long-term professional relationships.

Source. Person or organization that can suggest possible candidates to a recruiter during a search.

Specialist vs Generalist. Increasingly, clients demand a certain amount of industry or functional knowledge from the executive recruiter. Exclusive practices have sprung up in banking, healthcare, training, hi-tech, finance, etc. Yet there is always the demand, in addition (especially at higher executive levels), for the generalist viewpoint. How else, for example, can an executive with consumer products marketing experience in soft drinks be found for the personal computer company that has decided it needs this type of leadership?

Some industries lend themselves to recruiter specialization, i.e., those with a large number of non-competing units nationally (banks, hospitals). Others, with a high concentration of firms (automobiles, for example) do not lend themselves to specialization. The determinant is adherence to a professional Off Limits policy. See OFF LIMITS.

Stalking Horse.   A candidate submitted relatively early to test, confirm and fine-tune specifications. Not a uniform practice and frowned upon by some as unfair to the candidate.

Stick Rate.   Term sometimes used to describe effectiveness of executive-position matches, whether through search or otherwise. No real statistics yet on whether searched executives last longer in new posts. Not to be confused, however, with success rate (i.e., underperformers can sometimes stay in the job for a long time!).

Stopper.   When a search firm hears another search firm may get an assignment, it sends over a few resumes as "stoppers." See LOBBING.

Super-Executive.   Manager who combines the talents and experience of the two or three people he or she is replacing. See BUNDLING.

Suspect.   A person identified in a preliminary way as a possible candidate to fill a search assignment.

Total Compensation.   See COMPENSATION PACKAGE.

Types of Executive Recruiters.   These include independent individual recruiters and recruiting firms, executive recruiting divisions of management consultant firms and certified public accounting firms, and internal recruiting departments in companies.

Unbundling.   Separating the key elements of full search and offering them individually, i.e., research, interviewing, etc., sometimes "demanded" by aggressive clients, sometimes offered aggressively by entrepreneurial recruiters seeking additional revenues.

Unethical Research.   Certain practices, such as phone-sourcing and "research" techniques which involve misrepresenting the caller or purpose of the call, are unprofessional and are not tolerated by professional recruiters regardless of whether they are employed by subcontractors or the search consultant himself. Such practices undermine client confidence in the integrity and professional reliability of recruiters. See RUSING.

Available in booklet form. An option is also offered for customizing the booklet with an individual firm's logo and message on the back cover. Call or write:
Consultants Bookstore, Templeton Road, Fitzwilliam, NH 03447. (603) 585-6544

Professional Association

AESC
ASSOCIATION OF EXECUTIVE SEARCH CONSULTANTS, INC.

NOTE: This information was provided by AESC.

INTRODUCTION TO CODE OF ETHICS AND PROFESSIONAL PRACTICE GUIDELINES

The Association of Executive Search Consultants (AESC) is an association of leading retained executive search consulting firms worldwide. Dating from its inception in 1959, the AESC has sought to promote high standards of professionalism among retained executive search consultants. In furtherance of this aim, AESC adopted a Code of Ethics in 1977, and a set of Professional Practice Guidelines in 1984. In 1996, with the advice of a panel of AESC member firm leaders and outside experts, the AESC revised and updated both the Code and the Professional Practice Guidelines to reflect important developments in the profession and the business environment.

"Retained executive search consulting" is a specialized form of senior-level management consulting, conducted through an exclusive engagement and on a predetermined retainer-fee basis. Its purpose is to assist executives of a client organization in defining executive positions, identifying well-qualified and motivated candidates, and selecting those best suited through comprehensive, quality assured search processes.

Executive search is widely-recognized as an indispensable service to organizations worldwide and is generally built on relationships rather than discrete transactions. The services provided by executive search consultants are an integral part of the process of building and maintaining corporate, nonprofit and government clients. Like professionals in the fields of law, public accounting and general management consulting, executive search consultants have a profound influence on the organizations they serve.

AESC and its members recognize that outstanding professional service rests on the quality and integrity of relationships with clients, candidates, employees and the public. Executive search consulting firms depend on all of these groups for their continuing success, and to each group they have important responsibilities.

Clients

AESC members are partners with their clients in a consultative process aimed at selecting organizational leaders. As "leadership" can have many meanings, the professional search consultant identifies the client's specific needs and unique culture as essential elements in recruiting appropriate leaders for client organizations.

Candidates

AESC members maintain professional relationships with candidates and treat them with respect at all times. AESC members regard honesty, objectivity, accuracy and confidentiality as fundamental to their relationships with candidates.

Consultants

AESC members strive to attract and develop their own talent, building the knowledge and experience that will guide the profession into the future. Recognizing the importance of training and education to this process, AESC members provide opportunities for consultants, research professionals and other staff to improve their skills and capabilities. AESC and its member firms are partners in professional development.

The Public

AESC members understand the importance of public trust in the executive search profession. Professional search consultants stay abreast of socio-economic developments in the communities they serve and recognize the need to respond to contemporary developments such as changing demographics, new technologies and changes in the employment relationship. AESC's mission includes understanding these changes and taking constructive positions on public policy issues that affect the executive search profession, client organizations and the public.

The AESC's updated Code of Ethics clarifies the fundamental principles that guide executive search consultants in performing their duties and conducting their relationships with these constituencies. The Professional Practice Guidelines represent the AESC's view of contemporary best practices that exemplify the standards of professionalism expected of executive search consultants into the 21st Century. Underlying these principles and best practices is the expectation that AESC members will articulate and define clearly for clients the terms of their relationship and the members' commitment to perform their work professionally.

CODE OF ETHICS

The Association of Executive Search Consultants, Inc. (AESC) is a worldwide association of retained executive search consulting firms. In order to perform their duties responsibly, AESC member firms are guided by the following ethical principles, which reflect fundamental values of the retained executive search consulting profession. The AESC is committed to educating its members about the application of these principles.

	AESC members will:
Professionalism:	conduct their activities in a manner that reflects favorably on the profession.
Integrity:	conduct their business activities with integrity and avoid conduct that is deceptive or misleading.
Competence:	perform all search consulting assignments competently, and with an appropriate degree of knowledge, thoroughness and urgency.
Objectivity:	exercise objective and impartial judgment in each search consulting assignment, giving due consideration to all relevant facts.
Accuracy:	"strive to be accurate in all communications with clients and candidates and encourage them to exchange relevant and accurate information.
Conflicts of Interest:	avoid, or resolve through disclosure and waiver, conflicts of interest.
Confidentiality:	respect confidential information entrusted to them by clients and candidates.
Loyalty:	"serve their clients loyally and protect client interests when performing assignments.
Equal Opportunity:	support equal opportunity in employment and objectively evaluate all qualified candidates.
Public Interest:	conduct their activities with respect for the public interest.

PROFESSIONAL PRACTICE GUIDELINES

Preamble

The Association of Executive Search Consultants (AESC) strives to enhance the professionalism of its members. Accordingly, AESC has developed the following

Professional Practice Guidelines to assist AESC member firms in their business relationships with clients, candidates and the public. As the profession evolves and adapts to developments in business practices, technology and law, the AESC may amend these Guidelines.

Relationships between AESC Members and Their Clients

AESC members are partners with their clients in a consultative process aimed at selecting organizational leaders. The success of these partnerships depends on excellence in client service. The following guidelines describe the processes and professional practices that contribute to outstanding client service.

Accepting Client Assignments

Outstanding client service begins with a full understanding of the client organization, its business needs and the position to be filled. An AESC member should:

- Accept only those assignments that a member is qualified to undertake on the basis of the member's knowledge of the client's needs and the member's ability to perform the specific assignment.
- Accept only those assignments that will not adversely affect the member's objectivity, loyalty and integrity.
- Disclose to present and prospective clients information known to the member about relationships, circumstances or interests that might create actual or potential conflicts of interest, and accept potential assignments only if all affected parties have expressly agreed to waive any conflict.
- Disclose to present and prospective clients limitations arising through service to other clients that may affect the member's ability to perform the search assignment.
- Base acceptances on an understanding that, among other things, defines the scope and character of the services to be provided; the identity of the client organization; the period, if any, during which the member will not recruit from the defined client organization; and the fees and expenses to be charged for the services rendered.
- Discuss with the client when advertising is required by law or is a recommended strategy for the particular search assignment.

Performing Client Assignments

Members should serve their clients with integrity and objectivity, making every effort to conduct search consulting activities on the basis of impartial consideration of relevant facts. Specifically, an AESC member should:

- Conduct an appropriate search for qualified candidates.
- Advise the client promptly, and offer alternative courses of action if it becomes apparent that no qualified candidates can be presented, or that the length of the search will differ considerably from that originally specified.

- Present information about the client, the position, and the candidate honestly and factually, and include reservations that are pertinent and important to an assignment.
- Withdraw from the assignment if a member determines that a client has characterized its organization falsely or misled candidates, provided the situation is not rectified.
- Thoroughly evaluate potential candidates, including
- in-depth interviews in person or by video conferencing,
- verification of credentials, and
- careful assessment of the candidate's strengths and weaknesses, before presenting candidates for client interviews.
- Complete thorough reference checks and transmit these references to the client.
- Advise the client if advertising becomes necessary.
- Avoid the voluntary presentation of resumes in the absence of an existing client relationship.

Preserving the Confidentiality of Client Information

AESC members should use their best efforts to protect confidential information concerning their clients. Specifically, a member should:

- Use such confidential information received from clients only for purposes of conducting the assignment.
- Disclose such confidential client information only to those individuals within the firm or to potential candidates who have a need to know the information.
- Not use such confidential information for personal gain, nor provide inside information to third parties for their personal gain.

Avoiding Conflicts of Interest

AESC members should protect their integrity, objectivity and loyalty by avoiding conflicts of interest with their clients. For example, a member should:

- Refuse or withdraw from an assignment upon learning of conditions that impair the member's ability to perform services properly, including conflicts of interest that may arise during the assignment (unless all affected parties expressly agree to waive the conflict).
- Inform clients of business or personal relationships with candidates that might affect or appear to affect the member's objectivity in conducting the assignment.
- Not accept payment for assisting an individual in securing employment.
- Avoid knowingly presenting simultaneously, without disclosure to clients, the same candidate to more than one client.

Relationships between AESC Members and Candidates

Although a member's primary relationship is with the client, member firms seek also to establish professional relationships with candidates. These relationships should be characterized by honesty, objectivity, accuracy and respect for confidentiality. In building such relationships, a member should:

- Provide candidates with relevant and accurate information about the client organization and the position.
- Present to clients accurate and relevant information about candidates, and otherwise maintain the confidentiality of information provided by prospective and actual candidates.
- Encourage candidates to provide accurate information about their qualifications. Upon learning that a candidate has misled the client or member regarding his or her qualifications, the member should reject the candidate, unless the client, candidate and member agree that the candidacy should continue following disclosure of the facts.
- Advise prospects and candidates of the status and disposition of their candidacies in a timely fashion.
- Consider whether an individual's permission is needed before sharing his or her background information with a client and secure permission as necessary (permission should always be obtained if an executive's "resume" is submitted).
- Advise candidates of any limitations on a member firm's ability to advance them as candidates in future searches.

Relationships between AESC Members and Their Contractors

AESC members sometimes rely on contractors and subcontractors to assist in the search process. A member should:

- Avoid contractors and subcontractors whose practices are inconsistent with the standards of professionalism expected of AESC members.
- Encourage its contractors and subcontractors to adhere to the Code of Ethics and Professional Practice Guidelines.

Relationships between AESC Members and the Public

AESC members should recognize the importance of public trust and confidence in their profession and seek to serve their clients in a manner consistent with the public interest. There, a member should:

- Observe the principles of equal opportunity in employment and avoid unlawful discrimination against qualified candidates.

- Promote and advertise member firm services in a professional and accurate manner.
- Conduct relations with the media so as to reflect favorably upon the AESC, clients and the executive search consulting profession.

International Association of Corporate & Professional Resources, Inc.

IACPR

NOTE: This information was provided by IACPR.

We are a group of senior-level human resource executives, retained executive search professionals, and consultants working on key issues in our field. We strive to form long-lasting, career friendships. We meet face-to-face at chapters in world business capitals. All members meet qualifications based on experience and acceptance of our code of ethics.

POLICIES & GUIDELINES OF THE ASSOCIATION

Section 1. Membership Criteria

Membership in IACPR is limited to senior-level Human Resources executives and retained executive search consultants, whose current or primary responsibilities include executive search and who have at least ten years of relevant business experience. At the time of application for membership, the candidate must currently have responsibility for assigning or conducting searches for executive personnel. Individuals are only admitted or retained as members of IACPR if their personal recruiting practices, and/or the recruiting practices of individuals under their direction, include all of the actions listed below before candidates are proposed:

- Meet with the client or hiring manager to develop an understanding of the open position and of the person needed to fill it.
- Develop written specifications for approval.
- Conduct comprehensive research for qualified candidates.
- Evaluate potential candidates through in-depth personal interviews.
- Perform comprehensive reference checking.

IACPR takes the position that the above items are always necessary to the conduct of a professional search whether performed internally by corporate staff or externally by search consultants. All candidates are to be sponsored by four professional references, two of whom are current members of the Association.

Section 2. Professional Recruiting Guidelines

A. Purpose
To develop, establish and promote ethical standards and practices among the IACPR membership.

B. Privileged Information
It is vital to the executive search process that exchange of information between the search firm and the company be held in confidence. The Executive Search Consultant must have access to sensitive information such as organizational strengths and weaknesses, marketing plans, new product developments and strategic plans in order to set the benchmarks for qualifying candidates. The use of such information for any other purpose is prohibited. Similarly, company representatives must treat information from a search firm with confidentiality such as candidate profiles, search strategies, search firm policies and procedures, and data gleaned through candidate interviews.

C. Defined Limits
Executive Search Consultants will agree with the client what constitutes the "client organization" and will not recruit nor cause to be recruited any person from the defined organization for a mutually agreed upon period after the completion of an assignment for the client organization. Search firms are obliged to notify a prospective client in advance of any companies appropriate to the search that will not be used due to prior client obligations.

D. Reference Checking
A feeling of trust must be preserved and cultivated between an Executive Search Consultant and a potential candidate. Reference checking without the knowledge and permission of the candidate, while sometimes expedient, is nevertheless a disservice to the candidate, unprofessional and is also unlawful.

E. Discrimination
No members of IACPR will permit candidate discrimination based on age, sex, religion, race or country of origin or handicap, except when addressing an imbalance by affirmative action.

F. Professional Conduct
Each member of IACPR assumes responsibility for maintaining ethical standards and projecting an image of professionalism. Members should refrain from making derogatory comments that adversely affect the interest of the Association or individual members or which conflicts with the purpose and standards of the Association.

Section 3. Professional Recruiting Commitment to Candidates

- A candidate will be informed by the Executive Search Consultant of the role of the search firm in the assignment, the nature of the engagement, and how the search process is likely to evolve.
- A candidate has the right to accurate information from the search consultant and/or corporate recruiter, negative as well as positive, about the position, company, hiring executive, and business conditions.
- A candidate can expect confidentiality and discretion at all times. Specific information obtained by the search consultant during discussions with the candidate may not be disclosed to the client if the candidate specifically so requests.
- A candidate must be made aware, however, that the Executive Search Consultant can choose not to present a candidate based on a judgment that the candidate is not qualified or appropriate for the position.
- A candidate will be told by the Executive Search Consultant and/or corporate recruiter the title, specifications of the position, reporting relationship, location, background of the company, and responsibilities of the position prior to a first interview with the hiring executive.
- A candidate will be kept informed of the status of his or her potential candidacy on a timely and candid basis by the search consultant or corporate recruiter.
- A candidate should expect that the Executive Search Consultant and/or corporate recruiter, or another company executive will not check references without the candidate's approval or do anything that might otherwise jeopardize the candidate's present position.
- A candidate should be informed of the fact, when appropriate, that an offer may be contingent upon successful completion of reference checks, special testing or any other conditions of employment.
- A candidate should expect that an Executive Search Consultant and/or corporate recruiter will objectively communicate his opinion of the impact on the individual's career of joining the company in the specified position.
- A candidate who is not ultimately offered the position can expect that all files will be kept confidential by the Executive Search Consultant and/or corporate client. Resumes will not be sent to another client or elsewhere in the organization without the candidate's prior approval.
- A candidate will be informed promptly by the Executive Search Consultant and/or corporate recruiter of the client's selection decision.
- A candidate should expect to continue to communicate with the Executive Search Consultant and/or corporate recruiter for at least six months after joining the company to ensure that any adjustment problems on either side are properly handled.

Associations

AESC
ASSOCIATION OF EXECUTIVE SEARCH CONSULTANTS, INC.

Association of Executive Search Consultants/500 Fifth Ave., Ste. 930/New York, NY 10110-0900/212-398-9556. The professional body for search firms. About 100 members, including all the largest firms. Has referral and complaint procedures. List of member firms available, call for more information.

IACPR

International Association of Corporate and Professional Recruiters/1001 Green Bay Road, #308/Winnetka, IL 60093/847-441-1644. An organization of senior-level HR executives and retained executive search consultants, offering a meeting ground for buyer and seller of these services.

Other Useful Resources

The famous Red Book, published annually since 1971. Identifies thousands of executive search firms, both retainer and contingency. Indexed by management function, industry, geography and individual recruiter speciality. Also available on labels, CD-ROM and in report form.

Monthly newsletter described as the "bible of the executive search business." Timely, provocative, informative, ERN reveals the inner workings of executive recruiting. For search professionals as well as outsiders who have to deal with them. Kennedy Information/800-531-0007

The Directory of Legal Recruiters lists nearly 800 specialists in 320 firms and is indexed by 33 legal specialties, 22 industry focus areas and over 250 individual recruiter specialties as well as geographic locations. Detailed firm listings include descriptions, placement level, salary minimums and fee basis, providing all the information you need to locate the right firms. Kennedy Information/800-531-0007

320-page paperback profiles 225 firms in the U.S. and Europe. Function, industry, geography and key principal indexes, phone, fax and e-mail contacts, plus analysis of the market. Kennedy Information/800-531-0007